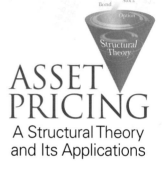

ASSET
PRICING
A Structural Theory
and Its Applications

Bond   Stock

Option

Structural
Theory

ASSET PRICING

A Structural Theory and Its Applications

BING CHENG
Chinese Academy of Science, China

HOWELL TONG
London School of Economics, UK

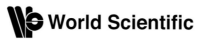

World Scientific

NEW JERSEY · LONDON · SINGAPORE · BEIJING · SHANGHAI · HONG KONG · TAIPEI · CHENNAI

Published by

World Scientific Publishing Co. Pte. Ltd.

5 Toh Tuck Link, Singapore 596224

USA office: 27 Warren Street, Suite 401-402, Hackensack, NJ 07601

UK office: 57 Shelton Street, Covent Garden, London WC2H 9HE

British Library Cataloguing-in-Publication Data
A catalogue record for this book is available from the British Library.

ASSET PRICING
A Structural Theory and Its Applications

ISBN-13 978-981-270-455-9
ISBN-10 981-270-455-8

Printed in Singapore by World Scientific Printers

Preface

Asset pricing theory plays a central role in finance theory and applications. Every asset, liability or cash flow has a value but an essential problem is, how to price it. In recent years, people even started talking about pricing an idea as an intangible asset! During the past half century, there appeared several methodologies to solve this problem. The first methodology is based on various economic partial (or general) equilibrium pricing models. Among these, the best known is Lucas' consumption-based asset pricing model. It links the asset pricing problem with the dynamical macro-economic theory. However, it is challenged by the well-known equity premium puzzle as pointed out by Mehra and Prescott in 1985. The issue is unresolved to-date. The second methodology is based on the so-called First Theorem in Finance due to Ross in 1976. Specifically, it values an asset by invoking the no-arbitrage principle in a complete capital market. This methodology/approach leads to, the well-known Arrow-Debreu security, the risk-neutral pricing, the APT (arbitrage pricing theory), and the equivalent-martingale measure. Interestingly, Sharpe's CAPM model can be derived from both methodologies referred to above. The third methodology involves the production-based pricing models. It links, in the long term, the firm economic growth theory with the asset pricing problem. In recent years, there has been a trend to unify the above methodologies and views under the title of stochastic discount factor (SDF) pricing models. Cochrane (2000) has summarized this trend.

In this book, we develop a new theory, which we call the Structural Theory, for asset pricing thereby putting the SDF pricing model firmly on a mathematical foundation. It includes a series of original results. Here we list some of the important ones. We separate the problem of finding a better asset pricing model from the problem of searching for "no equity" premium puzzle. The uniqueness theorem and the dual theorem of asset pricing indicate that, given market traded prices, a necessary and sufficient condition for the pricing functional space (or the SDF space) to have a unique *correctly pricing functional* (or *correctly pricing SDF*) is that, the space is isometric to the asset payoff space. The orthogonal projection operator, introduced in the dual theorem, provides a bijective and valuation-preserving mapping between the two spaces. A new explanation for the Mehra and Prescott's puzzle can be described as follows: (1) The structure of the consumption growth power space is not rich enough to provide an SDF which is capable of pricing every portfolio in the asset space correctly (*i.e.*, the two spaces are not isometric), within feasible ranges of the economic parameters. For example, when the risk aversion is chosen to be less than 5, a big pricing error appears. (2) In order to have no pricing error, given insufficient structure of the SDF space, the estimated parameter has to be exaggerated to an unreasonable level. For example, the risk aversion must be beyond 50 for the U.S market. The structure theory indicates that the appearance of the equity premium puzzle is *relative* and it depends on a matching (or rather a valuation-preserving isometric mapping) between an SDF space and an asset space. For matching pairs of the two spaces, there exists a unique SDF to price every portfolio in the asset space correctly. If the correctly pricing SDF is with sensible economic parameters, then there is no puzzle. However, if the correctly pricing SDF is with infeasible economic parameters, we say that the puzzle appears to this SDF space. Theoretically, given the asset space, we can remove this puzzle by enlarging the SDF space to one with sensible new economic parameters, for example, by adding new economic state variables to span a bigger SDF space rather than extending the range of the parameters in the original (smaller) SDF space to an unreasonable level. If the augmented SDF space is matched to the asset space, there is a new SDF that may provide the tool to price every portfolio in the asset space correctly, with the result that there is no pricing error and hence no puzzle to the asset space. Alternatively, given the SDF space, we may, by dropping some assets from the asset space, find a new correctly pricing SDF with sensible parameters to the reduced asset space, with the result that we would then see no pricing error and hence no puzzle to the reduced asset space. In general, mis-matching an SDF space with an asset space will definitely create some pricing error. The puzzle is in fact the result of an improper attempt to remove the pricing error. Using the above theory, it is easy to see why the Epstein-Zin model is less prone to cause the puzzle. The SDF space generated by the Epstein-Zin model is richer than the CRRA (constant-relative-risk aversion) based SDF space used by Mehra and Prescott in 1985. The Epstein-Zin SDF space is spanned by two state variables, namely the consumption growth and the market return. But the CRRA (constant-relative-risk aversion) based SDF space is only spanned by the single consumption growth state variable. So, within a relatively reasonable range of the parameters, the Epstein-Zin based model is capable of achieving a smaller pricing error for the same asset space.

The symmetric theorem of asset pricing provides a way to value non-tradable factors, such as economic indices, by reflexively using market assets and their corresponding market prices. The expanding theorem of asset pricing provides a bottom-up way to construct a correctly pricing SDF for an asset space. Based on correctly pricing SDFs for subspaces of the asset space and other covariance information, we can find a unique SDF, in a minimum complete expansion of the sum of SDF subspaces, to price whole portfolios in the asset space correctly. The compression theorem of asset pricing provides a top-down way to construct asset pricing models. To price well-diversified asset portfolios with K-factor structures correctly, a necessary and sufficient condition for an SDF space to have a unique correctly pricing SDF is that the SDF space possesses a K-factor structure as well. In other words, both spaces have no idiosyncratic risk and only K factor risks are left to be considered. Cochrane (2000) has used this fact without giving a rigorous proof. A combination of the expanding theorem and the compression theorem can provide a routine way to value portfolios at different levels. Based on the theory of corporate finance, the theory of interest rate and the theory of derivative pricing, the valuation of an individual security has been well developed. However, portfolio valuation, in particular, risk arbitrage portfolio valuation, well-diversified portfolio valuation or index valuation, is less well developed. The pricing error theorem of asset pricing indicates a way of measuring how well a given SDF does the pricing job, by first projecting it and the unknown correctly pricing SDF into the asset space, and then measuring the closeness between the two projected proxies by using, for example, the Hansen-Jagannathan distance. There are three possible sources of pricing errors: the difference in the means of the proxies, the difference in the volatilities of the two proxies, and the imperfect correlation between the two proxies. Empirical results suggest that the main contribution to the pricing error is the difference in volatility.

In a multi-period framework, we propose to link CPPI (constant proportion portfolio insurance) with Merton's consumption pricing model with minimal constraint on consumption.

Throughout this book, various real examples are used to illustrate ideas and applications in practice.

Finally, we are most grateful to the National Science Foundation of China for their support to Bing Cheng under the Risk Measurement Project (No. 70321001) and the Scientist Group on Uncertainty, and the London School of Economics and Political Science for granting Howell Tong a sabbatical term to work on the book. Bing Cheng wishes to thank his wife, Corin, for the assistance in preparing the figures in this book and for her support when he did the research in 2005 and wrote the book in 2007.

Contents

List of Figures

List of Tables

Chapter 1

Introduction to Modern Asset Pricing

1.1 A Brief History of Modern Asset Pricing Models

The history of asset pricing is more than three hundred years old but Modern Finance started only about half a century ago. It is generally accepted that Arrow's paper entitled *Optimal Allocation of Securities in Risk Bearing* in 1953 marked the starting point of Modern Finance. In 1874, the French economist, L. Warlas, introduced the concept of general equilibrium, making it the first notion of economic equilibrium in the history of economics study, which was followed by numerous contributions from many famous economists. It was only in 1954 that Arrow and Debreu finally gave a proof to the existence of a general equilibrium.

In Arrow's paper in 1953, he interpreted a financial security as a series of commodities in various future states with different values. This interpretation was later refined by Debreu, who incorporated an equilibrium model over a state space to deal with a financial market so that a security was nothing but a commodity with different values in different states and at different times. His notions of a state price and a state security (or Arrow security) are very popular now. All of these notions are based on the assumption of a complete financial market, that is, corresponding to each contingent state, there is an Arrow security to be traded in a financial market.

When it comes to stock investment, what is its utility? In his doctoral dissertation entitled *Theory of Investment Values* in 1937, William proposed an appraisal model of stock that asks investor to do a long-term forecast of a firm's future dividends and check the accuracy of the forecasting. Later, William described how to combine the forecasting with its accuracy to estimate the intrinsic value of a stock, leading to the well-known DDM (discount dividend model).

When Markowitz studied the DDM model, he found that if all investors follow a DDM model, they would all purchase the stock with the highest expected return and avoid other stocks. This was obviously counter-intuitive. So in his seminal paper in 1952, he proposed that investors need to consider a balance between the return and the risk; indeed he used the mean to describe the expected return and the variance to describe the risk. With this framework, he developed a mean-variance efficient frontier in that given the risk level, an optimal portfolio with the highest expected return is obtained, or equivalently given the expected return level, an optimal portfolio with the minimum risk is obtained. Based on this efficient frontier, the well known two-fund separation theorem was developed to help rational investors to develop optimal investment strategy.

In 1958, Tobin pointed out that when there is a riskless asset, the frontier becomes a straight line and an optimal portfolio is then a combination of a risky asset and the riskless asset. In the 1960s, with all investors having the same expectation, Sharpe, Lintner and Mossin developed the Capital Asset Pricing Model (CAPM) for a financial market at an equilibrium state. One of the important contributions from the CAPM is that it links excess return with the so-called market return. Merton in 1973 developed an Intertemporal Capital Asset Pricing Model, which links the excess return of a risky asset to not only the market return but also several state variables that will eventually result in multi-factors. In 1976, Ross proposed the Arbitrage Pricing Theory: given a financial market spanned by a number of factors, asset pricing of no-arbitrage is based on the results of the factor premiums and factor sensitivities.

In the 1970s, Lucas developed the consumption-based asset pricing model, and in the 1990s all the above models were merged into a more general pricing model, namely the stochastic discount factor (SDF) pricing model, which we discuss in detail as follows.

Modern consumption theory started in the 1930s, when Keynes in his famous book *The General Theory of Employment, Interest, and Money* proposed an Absolute Income Hypothesis based on the Fundamental Psychological Law. Specifically,

- there exists a stable functional relationship between real consumption and income;

- marginal propensity to consumption is bigger than 0 but less than 1;

- average propensity to consumption is decreasing along with increase of income.

Compared with Keynes' absolute income hypothesis, Duesenberry's relative income hypothesis in 1949 was an advancement. Duesenberry stressed the effect of consumption habit. Later, Modiglian and Brumberg (1954) proposed the Life Cycle Hypotheses and Friedman (1957) proposed the Permanent Income Hypotheses. The above work laid the foundation of modern consumption theory.

Modiglian and Brumberg assumed that there is a utility of aggregate consumption depending on historic and future consumption paths. Friedman (1957) divided income into two parts: a predictable income (called a permanent income) and an unpredictable income (called a temporary income). The Permanent Income Hypothesis claims that an individual consumption is not decided by the income of that period but by a life-long income i.e. the permanent income. The mathematical tools used by these authors were deterministic.

In the 1970s, there were two important events that influenced the development of the consumption theory: one is Lucas's (1976) critique on rational expectation and another is Hall's martingale model of consumption (1978). Both stressed expectation and uncertainty. Lucas argued that consumption depends on expected income and Hall proved that consumption follows a martingale process if the preference of the consumer is time-separable, the utility is of a quadratic form and the interest rate is constant. Hall's result shows that the Life Cycle Hypothesis and the Permanent Income Hypothesis follow a random walk. Let c_t denote the consumption at time t and E_t the conditional expectation given the information set up to time t. Then Hall's conclusion is

$$E_t c_{t+1} = c_t, \qquad (1.1)$$

or equivalently by using the representation of a martingale difference, a consumption dynamic process follows

$$c_{t+1} = c_t + \eta_{t+1} \qquad (1.2)$$

with η_{t+1} being a zero-mean normal white noise. Campbell and Cochrane (2000) stated, 'The development of consumption-based asset pricing theory ranks as one of the major advances in Financial Economics during the last two decades.' This comes from a very intuitive construction dealing with the tradeoff between investment and consumption. Specifically, let $e_{i,t}$ be the endowment of the *i-th* agent at time $t = 0, 1$, $c_{i,t}^j$ be his consumption of the *j-th* commodity (in physical unit or in monetary unit) at time $t = 0, 1$, $j = 1, 2, \cdots$. Let x_j be the payoff of a security which is a financial contract enforced among agents at time $t = 0$; the contract promises to pay back x_j units of commodity j at time $t = 1$. Here, x_j is often a random variable. The action of entering a financial contract is called an investment. Then a tradeoff is attained, for each agent, if endowment $e_{i,0}$ is allocated between the current consumption $c_{i,0}^j$ and the investment $w_{j,i}$, which is the number of contracts (bought or sold) for payoff x_j. People with great patience tend to consume less now and invest more. People with low risk aversion tend to be more involved in highly risky investments, in the hope of obtaining higher level of consumption in the future. The equilibrium allocation for each agent is to maximize his utility, given a budget constraint. Mathematically this is

$$\max_{\{w_{j,i}\}} \{E[u_i(c_0, c_1)]\} \tag{1.3}$$

with the budget constraint

$$c_0 = \sum_j c_{i,0}^j = e_{i,0} - \sum_j w_{i,j} p_j, \tag{1.4}$$

$$c_1 = \sum_j c_{i,1}^j = e_{i,1} + \sum_j w_{i,j} x_j, \tag{1.5}$$

where p_j is the price of the financial contract for commodity j at time $t = 0$, $u_i = u_i(c_0, c_1)$ is a utility function for agent i, and E is the expectation of a random variable. By a simple calculation, we derive an equation of the first condition for utility maximization - the so-called Euler equation:

$$p_j = E[IMRS_i x_j], \ j = 1, 2, \cdots, \tag{1.6}$$

where $IMRS_i$ is the inter-temporal marginal rate of substitution given by $IMRS_i = \frac{\partial u_i / \partial c_0}{\partial u_i / \partial c_1}$, where $\partial u_i / \partial c_i$, $i = 0, 1$, denotes the partial derivative of the utility with respect to the consumptions. The pioneers Lucas (1978), Breeden (1979), Grossman and Shiller (1981), and Hansen and Singleton (1982, 1983) studied the Euler equation in two ways: (i) To determine the assets' prices given the agent's utility function and the assets' payoffs; (ii) To determine, as an inverse problem, the parameters such as the risk aversion in

$IMRS$ by the GMM estimation procedure in Hansen and Singleton (1992, 1983), given the market prices and asset payoffs.

In recent years, people have started to consider a more general form of the Euler equation by introducing a random variable m satisfying

$$p = E[mx]. \tag{1.7}$$

Then m is called a stochastic discount factor (SDF). This framework includes the consumption-based asset models, the CAPM, the Ross arbitrage pricing theorem, the option pricing models and many other popular asset pricing models as special cases. For further details, the readers may wish to consult Cochrane (2001).

Alternatively m is called a state price density (SPD), which is a very popular name in the risk-neutral pricing world.

1.2 The Equity Premium Puzzle

The so-called risk premium is a monetary cost of uncertainty. Its general definition is as follows.

Definition 1.2.1 *Suppose we are given an initial wealth w_0 and investment $l = \langle p_1, x_1; p_2, x_2; \cdots ; p_n, x_n \rangle$, in which the investment has an outcome x_i with probability p_i, $i = 1, 2, \cdots, n$; here x_i could be money, a commodity or some other type. Let $w = w_0 + x$ be the terminal wealth. Let r be a real number satisfying*

$$u(Ew - r) = E[u(w)], \tag{1.8}$$

where $u(\cdot)$ is a utility function, E is the expectation, and $x = \{x_1, x_2, \cdots, x_n\}$. Then r is called the risk premium.

An intuitive interpretation of the risk premium is that an investor with utility u is indifferent to risky investment w and a deterministic investment (such as bank's deposit) with a fixed payoff $Ew - r$. To a risk averse investor, we expect that $r > 0$. By the no arbitrage principle, we can see $Ew - r = R_f$, where R_f is a risk-free interest rate. That is, for a risk averse investor to enter the risky trade w, the expected return of w must be higher than the risk-free interest rate by

$$Ew = R_f + r,$$

so r is an expected excess return to compensate the investor for entering the risky trading. When x is an equity, the risk premium becomes an equity

premium. It is the difference between the expected equity return and the
risk-free interest rate.

Mehra and Prescott (1985) announces a surprising discovery to the financial economics community, which later becomes the well-known *equity
premium puzzle*. The puzzle says that there exists a substantial difference
between the equity premium estimation by using the U.S. historical stock
market data and that by a slight variation of the Lucas model (1978) based
on the U.S. aggregate consumption data, unless the risk aversion parameter
is raised to an implausibly high level. In the above, we have described briefly
a justification for the consumption-based asset pricing modelling. Now, the
puzzle represents a serious challenge to the development of Financial Economics. Since its announcement, it has attracted the attention of many
financial economists. Specifically, Mehra and Prescott (1985) starts with
the problem of seeking an optimal solution for the following maximization
problem, which is a variation of the Lucas model (1978) in a pure exchange
economy:

$$\max_{c_t} E_0 \left[\sum_{t=0}^{\infty} \beta^t u(c_t) \right], \qquad 0 < \beta < 1, \tag{1.9}$$

subject to the budget constraints above, where β is a subjective discount
factor. The utility function is restricted to be of constant relative risk
aversion(CRRA) and takes the form

$$u(c) = \frac{c^{1-\gamma} - 1}{1 - \gamma}, \tag{1.10}$$

where γ is the coefficient of relative risk aversion. After some calculations,
the following Euler equation emerges

$$p_t = E_t \left[\beta \left(\frac{c_{t+1}}{c_t} \right)^{-\gamma} x_{t+1} \right], \tag{1.11}$$

where p_t is the market price at time t, x_{t+1} the stock's payoff at time $t+1$
with $x_{t+1} = p_{t+1} + d_{t+1}$, and d_{t+1} the stock's dividend.

Turning to empirical analysis, the paper finds that the average real
return on the riskless short-term securities over 1889-1978 period is 0.8%
and the average real return on the S&P 500 composite stock index over the
same period is 6.98% per annum. This leads to an average equity premium
of 6.18%. By varying γ between 0 and 10, and β between 0 and 1, they find
that it is not possible to obtain a matching sizable equity premium. The

largest premium from the simulation is only 0.35%! The paper concludes that their model of asset returns is inconsistent with the U.S. data on consumption and asset returns.

Given the market traded prices of some risky assets and the riskfree asset, the aim is to check if an SDF can price them correctly. Instead of checking the Euler equation directly, which is often complex, let m be the SDF that, according to the Euler equation, incurs no pricing error to the risky assets and the riskfree asset. Then Hansen and Jagannathan (1991) shows that there exists a relationship between m and the assets by introducing an upper bound for the so-called Sharpe ratio of the returns of risky assets, namely

$$\frac{|ER - R_f|}{\sigma_R} \leq SR^{max}, \tag{1.12}$$

where R is the (aggregate) return of the risky assets, ER the expectation of R, R_f the return of the riskfree asset, σ_R the volatility of R and SR^{max} the theoretically maximal Sharpe ratio. Here, $SR^{max} = \sigma_m/Em$, where σ_m is the volatility of m and Em the expectation of m. This latter ratio is called the Hansen-Jagannathan bound, or the H-J bound for short. There are two ways to exploit it. First, the absolute value of the Sharpe ratio of the return of risky assets has an upper bound given the SDF. In other words, any risky asset with a Sharpe ratio higher than the SR^{max} cannot be correctly priced (*i.e.* priced with no pricing error) by the SDF m. Alternatively, a necessary condition for an SDF candidate to be capable of pricing the assets correctly is that its SR^{max} must not violate a lower bound which is given by the maximum of the Sharpe ratios of the assets to be priced correctly. Either way the H-J bound provides us with a necessary and quick way to check whether the Euler equation is satisfied.

When the SDF m is given by the CRRA utility, we have $m = \beta(\frac{c_1}{c_0})^{-\gamma}$. Using the yearly U.S. economic and stock data, the inequality (1.12) is overwhelmingly violated, unless the risk aversion parameter γ reaches an extremely high level, say between 25 and 50 or even high. Mathematically, the puzzle can be stated as follow.

Given a series of payoffs $\{x_i\}$ for risky assets and their corresponding market prices $\{p_i\}$, let candidate SDF m be a series of SDFs given by $\{m = m_\theta, \ \theta \in \Theta\}$, where Θ is a parameter space in $\Re^L$. Let Θ_1 be a subspace of Θ whose range is feasible economically. For example, Θ can be defined by $\Theta = \{\gamma \mid 0 < \gamma < 1000\}$ and Θ_1 by $\Theta_1 = \{\gamma \mid 0 < \gamma < 5\}$. Then a 'parameterized' equity premium puzzle takes the form

$$p_i \neq E[m_\theta x_i] \text{ for some } i \text{ and } \forall \theta \in \Theta_1, \qquad (1.13)$$

but

$$p_i = E[m_\theta x_i] \text{ for all } i \text{ and for some } \theta \in \Theta. \qquad (1.14)$$

Hansen and Jagannathan (1997) introduces a distance to measure pricing errors for given asset pricing models. The distance becomes the well-known Hansen-Jagannathan distance. Both the H-J bound and the Hansen-Jagannathan distance are powerful ways to evaluate asset pricing models.

Kocherlakota (1996) points out that there are three possible ways to resolve the equity premium puzzle.

- Introduce progressively a more complex form of the utility function, e.g. by some judicious modification of the standard power utility function if time and state are separable, or by adopting a completely new form of the utility function if time and state cannot be separated.

- Traditional asset pricing models make the strong assumption that asset markets are complete, but the real world is not like that. Acknowledging that the market is incomplete in one's asset pricing model is one way to resolve the equity premium puzzle; this will be a new direction.

- Trading costs, such as taxes and brokerage fees, should be included in the asset pricing model because their effects on the equity premium cannot be ignored.

Mehra (2003) points out that the equity premium puzzle is a quantitative puzzle. The puzzle arises from the fact that a quantitative prediction of equity premium is much different from what has been historically documented. The puzzle cannot be dismissed lightly because our economic intuition is often based on our acceptance of models such as CCAPM (Consumption-based CAPM). Therefore, the validity of using such models for any quantitative assessment has also become an issue.

Over the past 20 years, attempts to resolve the puzzle have become a major research activity in Finance and Economics. Many different approaches have been adopted. These include, among many others, the recursive utility model by Epstein and Zin (1989,1991) and Weil (1989,1990), the habit formation model by Constatinides (1990), Abel (1990), and Campbell and Cochrane (1999), the three-state economy by Rietz (1988), the survivorship bias by Brown, Goetzmann, and Ross (1995), the idiosyncratic risk and incomplete markets considered by Mankiw (1986), Lucas (1994) and Telmer (1993), the generalized heterogeneous consumers specified by Constantinides and Duffie (1996) and Brav, Constantinides and Geczy (2002), the market imperfections models by Aiyagari and Gertler (1991), Alvarez and Jermann (2000), Bansal and Coleman (1996), Constantinides, Donaldson and Mehra (2002), Heaton and Lucas (1996), and McGrattan and Prescott (2001). In fact, hundreds of papers have been published in the Finance and Economics literature that are devoted to the puzzle. The puzzle is not only relevant to the foundation of the theory of Financial Economics but also crucial to the financial industry for such activities as the long-term asset allocation for pension funds, whose market size currently exceeds one trillion U.S. dollars. In the following, we give a brief introduction to some of the recent developments.

I. Preference Modifications

I.a Generalized Expected Utility

The standard preference class used in macroeconomics consists of time-and-state-separable utility functions. From the empirical analysis of Mehra and Prescott (1985), we know that the CRRA preference can match the observed equity premium only if the coefficient of relative risk aversion is implausibly large.

Epstein and Zin (1989,1991) present the notion of *generalized expected utility preference* (GEU) that allows independent parameterizations of the coefficient of risk aversion and the elasticity of inter-temporal substitution. The recursive utility, U_t, is given by

$$U_t = [c_t^{1-\rho} + \beta(E_t U_{t+1}^{1-\alpha})^{(1-\rho)/(1-\alpha)}]^{1/(1-\rho)}, \qquad (1.15)$$

where α measures the relative risk aversion and $1/\rho$ the elasticity of inter-temporal substitution. In contrast to the historical average risk premium of 6.2% and the largest premium obtained by Mehra and Prescott (1985) of 0.35%, Epstein and Zin's results in 1991 show a low riskfree rate and an average equity premium of roughly 2%. In their words, their GEU specification only partially resolves the puzzle. Weil's model in 1990 is very much like that in Epstein and Zin (1991). It is very interesting to note that the Epstein-Zin model gives a two-factor representation for the premium by

$$E_t r_{t+1} - r_{f,t+1} + \frac{\sigma_t^2}{2} = \frac{\theta}{\psi} cov_t(r_{t+1}, \Delta c_{t+1})$$

$$+ (1-\theta)cov_t(r_{t+1}, r_{p,t+1}). \qquad (1.16)$$

For detailed derivation, see, e.g., Campbell and Viceira (2002, p. 45). We shall give a new result later in the form of (Theorem (3.3.5)), which shows that this two-factor structure of the Epstein-Zin model is the key to the superior performance of the model over models of the CRRA type.

I.b Habit Formation

Abel (1990) and Constantinides (1990) consider the effects of consumption habit on the decision making of individuals. Constatinides specifies a utility as follows:

$$U(c) = E_t \sum_0^\infty \beta^s \frac{(c_{t+s} - \lambda c_{t+s-1})^{1-\alpha}}{1-\alpha}, \quad \lambda > 0, \qquad (1.17)$$

where λ is a parameter that captures the effect (or habit) of past consumption. This preference ordering makes individuals extremely averse to consumption risk even when the risk aversion is small.

Abel (1990) provides another kind of habit formation by defining utility of consumption relative to the average per capita consumption. The idea is that one's utility depends not only on the absolute level of consumption but also on how one is doing relative to others. In contrast to Constantinides (1990), the per capita consumption can be regarded as the 'external' habit formation for each individual. Again we shall give new results later to show why such a setup is to do with a more complex utility that goes back to Kocherlakota's point above.

Campbell and Cochrane (1999) specifies habit formation as external, similar to Abel (1990), and took the possibility of recession as a state variable so that a high equity premium could be generated.

As it turns out the habit formation models have only limited success as far as resolving the equity premium puzzle is concerned because effective risk aversion and prudence become improbably large in these models.

II. Incomplete Markets

Instead of assuming all the agents are homogeneous, Mankiw (1986) argues as follows. There are infinitely many consumers who are identical ex ante, but their consumptions are not the same ex post. The aggregate shocks to consumption are assumed to be not dispersed equally across all individuals but only affect some of them ex post. Under the assumption of incomplete markets, Mankiw shows that representative agent models are not effective as approximations to a complex economy with ex post heterogeneous individuals.

Lucas (1994) proposes a more general model than Mankiw (1986) by assuming undiversified shocks to income and borrowing, and short sale constraints at an infinite time horizon. In her model, individuals cannot insure, ex ante, against future idiosyncratic shocks to their income. She showed that individuals with a bad idiosyncratic shock can effectively self-insure by selling financial assets to individuals with good luck by trading. Hence, idiosyncratic risks to income are largely irrelevant to asset prices with trading even when the borrowing constraints are severe. To resolve the equity premium puzzle requires more than closing forward market for labour income. Telmer (1993) considers much a similar incomplete market model as Lucas (1994) by assuming two heterogeneous consumers with different consumption stream in the economy. His research supports Lucas' conclusion.

Constantinides and Duffie (1996) assumes that consumers are heterogeneous because of uninsurable, persistent and heteroscedastic labour income shocks at each time period. The paper constructs a model in which the Euler equations depend on not only the marginal rate of substitution (MRS) at the aggregate level but also the cross-sectional variance of the individual consumption growth. Continuing the work of Contandinides and Duffie (1996), Brav, Constantides and Geczy (2002) considers the case of asset pricing with heterogeneous agents and limited participation of households in capital markets. Their empirical analysis reveals that relaxation of the assumption of complete consumption insurance is helpful in resolving the equity premium puzzle.

III. Liquidity Premium and Trading Costs

Bansal and Coleman (1996) gives a monetary explanation for the equity premium puzzle. In their model, assets other than money play a key feature by facilitating transactions. Using empirical evidence, the paper claims that half of the equity premium can be captured by their model. Some economists try to explain the equity premium puzzle via transaction costs. For example, McGrattan and Prescott (2001) proposes an explanation based on changes in tax rates. Heaton and Lucas (1996) finds that the differences in trading costs across stocks and bond markets have to be very high in order to resolve the equity premium puzzle with transaction costs. Kocherlakota (1996) even shows that to match the real equity premium, the trading cost have to be implausibly high.

Mehra (2003) gives a comprehensive summary of recent developments; the puzzle remains open.

Chapter 2

A Structural Theory of Asset Pricing and the Equity Premium Puzzle

In this chapter we introduce a new theory of asset pricing, which we call the structural theory. Applying it to the equity premium puzzle, we shall be able to see when the puzzle is a puzzle and when it is not.

2.1 Construction of Continuous Linear Pricing Functionals and No-arbitrage Conditions

Let (Ω, F, P) be a probability space and $H = L^2(\Omega, F, P)$ be a contingent claim space. Let $\{x_1, x_2, \cdots, x_n, \cdots\}$ be a sequence of random payoffs in H. Let $\Im_n$ be the linear space spanned by $x_1, \cdots, x_n$ in H. Let $\Im = \cup_{n=1}^{\infty} \Im_n$, so that any x in $\Im$ is a random portfolio return from some finite subset of the assets. Let $\bar{\Im}$ be the closure of $\Im$ in H. It is well known that H is a Hilbert space, separable or not separable, under the inner product $< x, \ y >= E[xy]$. Therefore the asset payoff space (or the asset space for short) $\bar{\Im}$ is a Hilbert space as well by recalling the fact that any closed linear subspace in a Hilbert space is still a Hilbert space. For $n \geq 1$, let Σ_n be the covariance matrix of $x^n = (x_1, \cdots, x_n)$ and we assume that Σ_n is non-singular. Therefore Σ_n is positive-definite. Given payoffs $x_1, \cdots, x_n$, a Gram-Schmit orthogonalization procedure leading to $e_1, \cdots, e_n$ is given by

$$
\begin{cases}
\quad\quad y_1 = x_1 \text{ and setting } e_1 = x_1/||y_1|| \\
y_2 = x_2 - < x_2, e_1 > e_1 \text{ and setting } e_2 = y_2/||y_2|| \\
\quad\quad\quad\quad\quad\quad \cdots \\
y_n = x_n - \sum_{i=1}^{n-1} < x_n, e_i > e_i \text{ and setting } e_n = y_n/||y_n||.
\end{cases}
\tag{2.1}
$$

The sequence $e_1, \cdots, e_n$ has the property that $< e_i, e_j >= 0$ for $i \neq j$ and $< e_i, e_i >= ||e_i||^2 = 1$ for $i = 1, \cdots n$. Interested readers may consult Lax (2002, Chapter 6) for more detail.

Lemma 2.1.1 *The linear subspace $\Im_n$ is spanned by the orthonormal basis $\{e_1, \cdots, e_n\}$, in which Σ_n^e, the covariance matrix of $\{e_1, \cdots, e_n\}$, is nonsingular if and only if Σ_n is nonsingular.*

Proof: We prove sufficiency first. When Σ_n is nonsingular, we know that for each x_i, $< x_i, x_i >= ||x_i||^2 > 0$ because otherwise Σ_n is singular. Similarly if $y_i = 0$ for some i, then x_i is linearly dependent on $x_1, \cdots, x_{i-1}$. This implies that Σ_n is singular. We must have $||y_i|| > 0$ for $i = 1, \cdots n$. Therefore we can use the Gram-Schmit orthogonalization procedure above to produce an orthonormal base $e_1, \cdots, e_n$ for $\Im_n$, satisfying

$$
(e_1, \cdots, e_n)^T = A_n (x_1, \cdots, x_n)^T,
\tag{2.2}
$$

where T refers to the usual transpose operation in matrix algebra. $A_n = (a_{i,j})$ has the property

$$
a_{i,j} = \begin{cases} 0 & \text{if } j > i \\ 1/||x_i|| & \text{if } i = j. \end{cases}
\tag{2.3}
$$

We turn to necessity next. If $\Im_n$ is spanned by an orthonormal basis $\{e_1, \cdots, e_n\}$, there are two matrices A and B satisfying $(e_1, \cdots, e_n)^T = A_n (x_1, \cdots, x_n)^T$ and $(x_1, \cdots, x_n)^T = B_n (e_1, \cdots, e_n)^T$. Hence $(e_1, \cdots, e_n)^T = A_n B_n (e_1, \cdots, e_n)^T$. By the orthogonality of $e_1, \cdots, e_n$, we have $A_n B_n = I$, where I is the $n \times n$ identity matrix. We have $\Sigma_n = B_n \Sigma_n^e B_n^T$. Since both B and Σ_n^e are nonsingular, Σ_n is nonsingular.

$$\text{Q.E.D.}$$

Lemma 2.1.2 *Let $\{e_1, \cdots, e_n, \cdots\}$ be the orthonormal payoffs generated from the Gram-Schmit orthogonalization procedure above. Let H_1 denote* *the space $\{x \in H \mid x = \sum_{i=1}^{\infty} a_i e_i, \sum_{i=1}^{\infty} a_i^2 < \infty\}$. Then we have $\bar{\Im} = H_1$. In other words, $\bar{\Im}$ is spanned by the orthonormal base $\{e_1, e_2, \cdots e_n, \cdots\}$. Furthermore let $S = \{x \mid x = \sum_{i=1}^{\infty} a_i x_i$ with $\sum_{i=1}^{\infty} a_i^2 < \infty\}$. Then S is a linear subspace of $\bar{\Im}$.[1]*

Proof: Obviously H_1 is a Hilbert space. For each x in H_1 with $x = \sum_{i=1}^{\infty} a_i e_i$, define $x^n = \sum_{i=1}^{n} a_i e_i$. By Lemma 2.1.1, $x^n \in \Im_n$. Hence $x = \lim_{n \to \infty} x^n \in \bar{\Im}$. Therefore $H_1 \subset \bar{\Im}$. On the other hand, if there exists an $x \in \bar{\Im}$ but $x \notin H_1$, then since H_1 is a closed subspace of $\bar{\Im}$, we have $x = y + \epsilon$ with $y \in H_1$, $\epsilon \in \bar{\Im} - H_1$, and $\epsilon \neq 0$. Then, for $i = 1, 2, \cdots$, $< \epsilon, e_i >= 0$. However, since $\epsilon \in \bar{\Im}$, there is a vector ϵ^n in $\Im_n$ satisfying $\lim_{n \to \infty} \epsilon^n = \epsilon$. Since $\epsilon^n = \sum_{i=1}^{n} a_i e_i$, $< \epsilon, \epsilon^n >= \sum_{i=1}^{n} a_i < \epsilon, e_i >= 0$, therefore $< \epsilon, \epsilon >= \lim_{n \to \infty} < \epsilon, \epsilon^n >= 0$. This implies $\epsilon = 0$, which is a contradiction. Thus, we must have $\bar{\Im} \subset H_1$. Hence, we have $\bar{\Im} = H_1$. Let $x \in S$ with $x = \sum_{i=1}^{\infty} a_i x_i$ and define $x^n = \sum_{i=1}^{n} a_i x_i$. Then $x^n \to x$ in H. On the other hand, by Lemma 2.1.1, $x^n \in \Im_n$ and since $\bar{\Im}$ is closed, we obtain $x \in \bar{\Im}$. Hence $S \subset \bar{\Im}$.

Q.E.D.

Definition 2.1.3 Pricing Functional: *Let I be an ordered set such as $I = \{1, \cdots, n\}$, or $I = \{1, 2, \cdots\}$. Let $\{x_i, i \in I\}$ be a sequence of payoffs from the assets and $\{p_i, \ i \in I\}$ be a corresponding sequence of observed market prices in the asset market. Then a pricing functional π is a mapping from $S_I = span\{x_i, \ i \in I\} = \{x \mid x = \sum_{i \in I} w_i x_i$ with $\sum_{i \in I} w_i^2 < \infty\}$ to $\Re$ (the real line) given by*

$$\pi(x) = \{p \mid p = \sum_{i \in I} p_i w_i \text{ in } l^2 \text{ for some} \tag{2.4}$$

$$w \in l^2 \text{ such that } x = \sum_{i} w_i x_i \text{ in } H. \tag{2.5}$$

Definition 2.1.4 Law of One Price: *All portfolios with the same payoff have the same price. That is,*

$$\text{if } \sum_{i \in I} w_i x_i = \sum_{i \in I} w_i' x_i \text{ then } \sum_{i \in I} w_i p_i = \sum_{i \in I} w_i' p_i. \tag{2.6}$$

for any two portfolios $w = \{w_i, \ i \in I\}$ and $w' = \{w_i', \ i \in I\}$.

---

[1] We will have $S = \bar{\Im}$ only under very stringent conditions.

Lemma 2.1.5 *The Law of One Price holds if and only if the pricing functional π is a linear functional on S_I.*

Proof: If the Law of One Price holds, then the mapping π is single valued. To prove linearity, consider payoffs $x, x' \in S_I$ such that $x = \sum_{i \in I} w_i x_i$ and $x' = \sum_{i \in I} w'_i x_i$ for some portfolios w and w'. For arbitrary $a, b \in \Re$, then payoff $ax + bx' = (ax_i + bx'_i, \ i \in I)$ can be generated by the portfolio $aw + bw' = (aw_i + bw'_i, \ i \in I)$ with the price $p(aw + bw') = \sum_{i \in I} p_i(aw_i + bw'_i) = a\sum_{i \in I} p_i w_i + b\sum_{i \in I} p_i w'_i$. Because π is single valued, we have

$$\pi(ax + bx') = p(aw + bw') = apw + bpw' = a\pi(x) + b\pi(x').$$

Thus π is linear. Conversely, if π is a linear functional, then the Law of One Price holds by definition.

Q.E.D.

The continuity of π is linked to no-arbitrage. Kreps (1981) gives a relationship between arbitrage and continuity of π in a very general setting. Here we use Chamberlain and Rothschild's no-arbitrage assumption (1983, assumption A (ii)).

Assumption 2.1.1 *Let x^n be a sequence of finite portfolios in $\Im$. Let $V(x^n)$ denote the variance of x^n and $E(x^n)$ the expectation of x^n. If $V(x^n) \to 0$, $\pi(x^n) \to 1$, and $E(x^n) \to \alpha$, then $\alpha > 0$.*

Lemma 2.1.6 *If Assumption 2.1.1 holds, then π is continuous.*

We omit the proof, which is straightforward, but refer to Chamberlain and Rothschild (1983, Proposition 1).

Since π is continuous on $\Im$, it is easy to prove that π is bounded on $\Im$. Then according to the Hahn-Banach Theorem (e.g. Lax 2002, Chapter 3), π can be extended to a bounded linear functional $\tilde{\pi}$ on H such that on $\Im$, $\tilde{\pi} \equiv \pi$. Hence by the Riesz Representation Theorem (e.g. Lax 2002, Chapter 6), there is a unique element $m \in H$ satisfying

$$\forall x \in H, \ \tilde{\pi}(x) = <m, \ x> = E[mx]. \tag{2.7}$$

Since $\bar{\Im}$ is a closed linear subspace of H, we have an orthogonal decomposition such that

$$m = x^* + m_1 \text{ where } x^* \in \bar{\Im} \text{ and } m_1 \perp \bar{\Im}. \tag{2.8}$$

Therefore we have $\forall x \in \Im$,

$$\pi(x) = \tilde{\pi}(x) = <m, x> = <x^*, x> = E[x^* x]. \tag{2.9}$$

Since $\tilde{\pi}$ is a continuous extension of π, in the following, we will omit the notation $\tilde{\pi}$ and use simply π only.

Clearly m is a stochastic discount factor (SDF). In the following, we will use the following terms and acronyms interchangeably: pricing functional, SDF, state price density and SPD.

2.2 The Structural Theory of Asset Pricing – Part I

Given the traded prices of assets in a market, the popular steps to search a proper SDF are as follows. First, a family of SDF candidates $\{SDF(\theta)\}_{\theta \in \Theta}$ is formed, where Θ is a parameter space. For example, in the constant relative risk aversion (CRRA)'s case, $SDF(\theta) = IRMS(g_c, \lambda, \beta)$, where g_c is the growth of the aggregate consumption, λ the risk aversion parameter and β an impatience parameter. Second, some estimation method, such as the GMM estimation procedure, is used to estimate the parameters. Hansen and Singleton's treatment (1982) for the CRRA model is an example. In section 1, we demonstrated that $\lambda \approx 30$, which led to the so-called equity premium puzzle.

Now, we first define what we really mean by correct pricing and then discuss conditions which determine whether correct pricing will result or not.

Let $X = \Im_n$ or $X = \bar{\Im}$ according as the asset space for assets is finite or infinite. Let $p = \{p_1, \cdots, p_n\}$ or $p = \{p_1, \cdots, p_n, \cdots\}$ be the market price vector depending on whether we have a finite number of assets or an infinite number of assets. Let π denote the linear continuous functional on X satisfying

$$p_i = \pi(x_i) \text{ with } p_i \neq 0 \text{ for } i = 1, 2, \cdots,^2 \tag{2.10}$$

and for each i. Here we assume that p_i cannot be obtained through pricing a portfolio of the payoffs $\{x_j\}$ other than x_i, that is they satisfy the parsimoniously pricing condition

$$\forall x \in span\{x_1, \cdots, x_{i-1}, x_{i+1}, \cdots, x_n\}, \ p_i \neq \pi(x). \tag{2.11}$$

---

[2]$p_i = 0$ means that a free contract is allowed. Here we assume that no free contract exists in the asset market.

Definition 2.2.1 *Under the above setup, π is called a correctly pricing functional (CPF) for the asset space X, given the market prices. Let m be an SDF. If the pricing functional π (i.e., $\forall x \in X$, $\pi(x) = E[mx]$) induced by m is a CPF, then m is called a correctly pricing SDF.*

Obviously, a CPF to an asset space with feasible economic parameters will mean there is no equity premium puzzle for the asset space. According to the definition, a CPF and a correctly pricing SDF are equivalent notions.

Define an inner product in the dual space X^* of X by $< \pi, \pi' > = < x^*, (x^*)' >$, where x^* and $(x^*)'$ are the Riesz representations in X of π and π' respectively. It is well known that X^* is a Hilbert space. (See Lax (2002) for example.)

Assumption 2.2.1 *When $X = \bar{\Im}$, $\lim_{n \to \infty} \sum_{i=1}^{n} w_{i,n}^2 < \infty$, where $w^n = (w_{1,n}, \cdots, w_{n,n})^T$ for $n \geq 1$ given by the equation $w^n = A_n p^n$, A_n is the Gram-Schmit orthogonalization matrix in (2.3) and p^n is the market price vector $p^n = (p_1, \cdots, p_n)^T$.*

Lemma 2.2.2 Existence of CPF *These is a unique correctly pricing SDF in X, with the understanding that Assumption 2.2.1 applies if $X = \bar{\Im}$.*

Proof: First consider the case $X = \Im_n$. Select an $m \in X$ such that

$$p_i = E[mx_i], \ i = 1, \cdots n. \tag{2.12}$$

Since $m = \sum_{j=1}^{n} w_j e_j$, $p_i = \sum_{j=1}^{n} w_j E[e_j x_i]$. Since $x_i = \sum_{k=1}^{n} b_{i,k} e_k$, where $B_n = A_n^{-1}$ and A_n is the Gram-Schmit orthogonalization matrix in (2.3), we obtain $p_i = \sum_{j=1}^{n} b_{i,j} w_j$. Let $p^n = (p_1, \cdots, p_n)^T$ and $w^n = (w_1, \cdots, w_n)^T$. Then $p^n = B_n w^n$. Therefore if we let

$$w^n = A_n p^n, \tag{2.13}$$

then $m = \sum_{j=1}^{n} w_j e_j$ is a correctly pricing SDF in X. The above argument also indicates that for any correctly pricing SDF in X, it must always follow equation (2.13). This mean that it is unique. For the case $X = \bar{\Im}$, define an SDF $m^n = \sum_{k=1}^{n} w_{k,n} e_k$, where $w^n = (w_{1,n}, \cdots, w_{n,n})^T$ is given by (2.13). Under Assumption (2.2.1) and since X is complete, we see that m^n converges to an $m \in X$. For each $i \geq 1$, let $n \geq i$. We have $E[m^n x_i] = p_i$ by using (2.12) and (2.13). Letting $n \to \infty$, we obtain $E[mx_i] = p_i$ for $i = 1, 2, \cdots$. So m is a correctly pricing SDF in X. If there is another m' in X which is also correctly pricing, then $E[m e_j] = E[m' e_j]$, $j = 1, 2, \cdots$

since each e_j is a linear combination of $\{x_i\}$. $\forall x \in X$, $x = \sum_{j=1}^{\infty} w_j e_j$. Hence $E[mx] = E[m'x]$. By letting $x = m - m'$, we have $E[m - m']^2 = 0$. Then $m = m'$ in X. Therefore the correctly pricing SDF m is unique in X.

Q.E.D.

We have the first main result of the structural theory in the form of the following theorem.

Theorem 2.2.3 (Uniqueness Theorem of the minimum correctly pricing functional space) *Let X^* be the dual space of X, that is, X^* is the set of all linear continuous functionals on X. Suppose F is a closed and linear subspace of X^*. Then F has a unique correctly pricing functional (CPF) if and only if $F \equiv X^*$ subject to the understanding that if $X = \bar{\Im}$, Assumption 2.2.1 applies.*

Proof: Consider the necessary condition first. For all $x \in X$, either $x = \sum_{j=1}^{n} a_j e_j$ or $x = \sum_{j=1}^{\infty} a_j e_j$ since $X = \Im_n$ or $X = \bar{\Im}$. For simplicity of notation, we denote $x = \sum_j a_j e_j$. From Lemma 2.2.1, let $\{e_j\}$ be the orthonormal base of X. Define a linear pricing functional π_j by

$$\forall x \in X, \ \pi_j(x) = E[e_j x]. \tag{2.14}$$

It is easy to see that $< \pi_i, \pi_j > = < e_i, e_j > = 0$ if $i \neq j$ and $< \pi_i, \pi_i > = < e_i, e_i > = 1$. Suppose that π is a pricing functional satisfying $< \pi, \pi_j > = 0$ for all j. Then $\forall x = \sum_j a_j e_j \in X$, $\pi(x) = E[x^* x] = \sum_j a_j E[x^* e_j] = \sum_j a_j < \pi, \pi_j > = 0$, where x^* is the Riesz Representation of π in X. This implies that $\pi = 0$. We obtain that $\{\pi_j\}$ is an othornormal base for X^*. Suppose that π is a CPF. Then we have

$$\pi = \sum_j a_j \pi_j, \tag{2.15}$$

in X^*. If $F \neq X^*$, then there exists a π_{j_0} satisfying $\pi_{j_0} \notin F$. By the representation in (2.15), $\pi = \sum_{j, j \neq j_0} a_j \pi_j$. Hence $\pi(e_{j_0}) = \sum_{j, j \neq j_0} a_j \pi_j(e_{j_0}) = 0$. Using the Gram-Schmit orthogonalization equation (2.1), we have $p_{j_0} = \pi(x_{j_0}) = \sum_{i=1}^{j-1} c_i \pi(x_i) = \pi(\sum_{i=1}^{j-1} c_i x_i)$. However, this violates the assumption of the parsimoniously pricing condition (2.11). We must therefore have $\pi(e_{j_0}) \neq 0$. This is a contradiction. Thus, $F \equiv X^*$.

We turn to sufficiency next. On using Lemma 2.2.1, there is a unique correctly pricing SDF m in X. Let pricing functional π be induced by m.

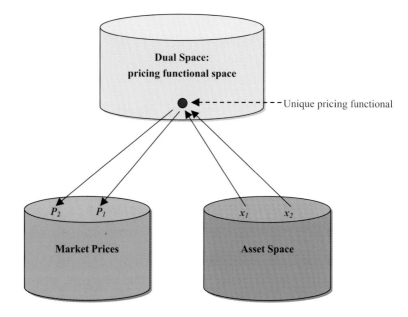

Figure 2.1: The Uniqueness Theorem of the minimum correctly pricing functional space.

That is $\forall x \in X, \pi(x) = E[mx]$. Then π is a CPF in $F = X^*$. Suppose there are two CPFs, say π_1 and π_2, in F. When $X = \Im_n$, since $\pi_1(x_i) = \pi_2(x_i)$ for $i = 1, \cdots, n$ and $\Im_n = span\{x_1, \cdots, x_n\}$, we have $\pi_1 = \pi_2$ in F. When $X = \bar{\Im}$, $\forall x \in X$, let $x^n \in \Im_n$ satisfy $x^n \to x$ in X. Since $\pi_1(x^n) = \pi_2(x^n)$, by letting $n \to \infty$, we have $\pi_1(x) = \pi_2(x)$. Hence $\pi_1 = \pi_2$ in F.

Q.E.D.

The implication of Theorem (2.2.3) is that, in order to price correctly, we need to search those pricing functionals in a candidate space that is isometric to a corresponding linear continuous pricing functional space. Note that a proper subspace of the linear pricing functional space does not contain a CPF. See Figure 2.1 for an illustration.

Very often, we use some SDFs or state price densities in the claim contingent space H to form a candidate space of pricing kernels. We introduce the following definition.

Let M be an SDF linear subspace in H. Let asset space $X = \Im_n$ or $\bar{\Im}$. Let T be an orthogonal projection operator from M to X, that is,

$\forall m \in M$, $T(m) \in X$ such that $\forall x \in X$, $E[(m - T(m))x] = 0$. We denote it by $T(m) = \hat{E}[m|X]$.[3]

Obviously the orthogonal projection operator preserves the original valuation, namely $\forall x \in X, m \in M$, $E[mx] = E[T(m)x]$. We are now ready to state the second main result.

Theorem 2.2.4 (Dual theorem for correctly pricing SDF space and asset payoff space) *M has a unique correctly SDF if and only if the orthogonal operator T is a continuous linear bijective operator from M to X, subject to the understanding that if $X = \widetilde{\mathfrak{S}}$, then Assumption 2.2.1 applies.*

Proof: We start with the necessity. $\forall m \in M$, define a linear functional π_m by $\forall x \in X$, $\pi_m(x) = E[mx]$. Since M has a unique correctly pricing SDF, there is a unique CPF in $F = \{\pi_m | m \in M\}$. According to Theorem 2.2.2, $F = X^*$. So $\forall y \in X$, define a linear continuous functional π_y by $\forall x \in X$, $\pi_y(x) = E[yx]$. Since $X^* = F$, there exists a $\pi_{m_y} \in F$ such that $\pi_y = \pi_{m_y}$. In other words, $\forall x \in X$, $E[yx] = E[m_y x]$. Now we define a mapping S from X to M by

$$S : y \in X \to m_y \in M. \tag{2.16}$$

First we show that S is a single-valued mapping. Suppose there are two mappings, say m_y and m'_y, satisfying $\forall x \in X$, $E[yx] = E[m_y x]$ and $E[yx] = E[m'_y x]$. This implies that $E[(m_y - m'_y)x] = 0$, $\forall x \in X$. This means that $m_y - m'_y \perp X$. Let m_0 be the correctly pricing SDF in M. Then we know that $m_0 + (m_y - m'_y)$ is also correctly pricing for X. By the uniqueness of correctly pricing SDF, we have $m_y - m'_y = 0$. Hence S is a single-valued mapping. Secondly we show that S is surjective. $\forall m \in M$, we have $\pi_m \in F = X^*$. Using the Riesz Representation Theorem, there is an $x_m \in X$ satisfying $\forall x \in X$, $E[mx] = \pi_m(x) = E[x_m x]$. Again by the uniqueness of correctly pricing SDF, we have $S(x_m) = m_{x_m} = m$. Hence S is surjective. Suppose that $y, z \in X, y \neq z$, $m_y = m_z$. This means that $\forall x \in X$, $E[(y - z)x] = E[(m_y - m_z)x] = 0$. Let $x = y - z$. Then $E[y - z]^2 = 0$, which means that $y = z$. This is a contradiction. So, S must be injective. Hence S is bijective. Since for any two real numbers a and b, $\forall x \in X, E[(ay + bz)x] = aE[yx] + bE[zx] = E[(am_y + bm_z)x]$. We can see that S is linear. $\forall m \in M$ and $\forall x \in X$, $E[mx] = E[S^{-1}(m)x]$. That is $E[(m - S^{-1}(m))x] = 0, \forall x \in X$.

---

[3] An orthogonal operator does not have to be a conditional expectation operator.

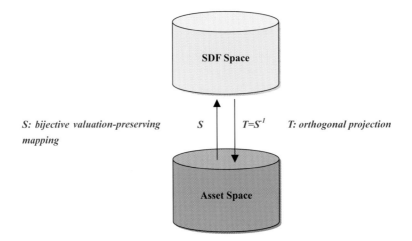

Figure 2.2: The Dual Theorem between an SDF Space and an asset payoff space.

This means that S^{-1} is the orthogonal operator from M to X. Therefore $T = S^{-1}$. Clearly T is linear. Let $m_k \to m$ in M as $k \to \infty$. For continuity of T, we need to show that $T(m_k) \to T(m)$ in X as $k \to \infty$. By the orthogonality of T, $\forall x \in X$, $E[(m_k - m)x] = E[(T(m_k) - T(m))x]$. Let $x = T(m_k) - T(m)$. Then we have $E[T(m_k) - T(m)]^2 = E[(m_k - m)(T(m_k) - T(m))] \le \sqrt{E[m_k - m]^2}\sqrt{E[T(m_k) - T(m)]^2}$ by the Cauchy-Schwartz Inequality. Hence $\sqrt{E[T(m_k) - T(m)]^2} \le \sqrt{E[m_k - m]^2}$. This implies that T is continuous and $||T|| = 1$, completing the proof of necessity.

We turn to sufficiency next. We have the existence of a unique correctly pricing SDF in X from Lemma (2.2.2). Then we use operator S to map it into space M. Hence there is one correctly pricing SDF in M. The uniqueness of correctly pricing SDF in M follows from the injective condition of the operator T and Lemma (2.2.2).

Q.E.D.

2.3   Is the Equity Premium Puzzle Really a Puzzle or not a Puzzle?

The implications of Theorem (2.2.3) and Theorem (2.2.4) are very important. They indicate that, given market traded prices, a necessary and sufficient condition for the pricing functional space (or the SDF space)

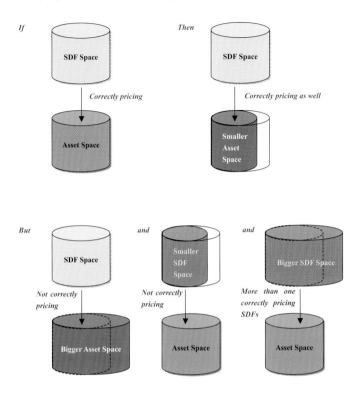

Figure 2.3: Implication of the Dual Theorem.

to have a unique *correctly pricing functional* (or *correctly pricing SDF*) is that the space is isometric to the asset space. The orthogonal projection operator, introduced in the dual theorem, provides a bijective and valuation-preserving mapping between the two spaces. See Figure 2.3 for an illustration.

The structural theory indicates that whether there is an equity premium puzzle or not is *relative*; it depends on the existence of a matching (i.e. a valuation-preserving isometric mapping) between an SDF space and a related asset space. For matching pairs, there always exists a unique SDF to price correctly every portfolio in the asset space. If the correctly pricing SDF is with sensible economic parameters, then there is no puzzle. However if the correctly pricing SDF is with infeasible economic parameters, we say that the puzzle appears in respect of this SDF space. Theoretically, given the asset space, we can remove the puzzle by enlarging the SDF space

to one with sensible new economic parameters, for example, by augment-
ing new economic state variables to span a bigger SDF space rather than
by extending the range of the parameters in the original SDF space to an
unreasonable level. If the augmented SDF space is matched to the asset
space, we may find a new SDF to price correctly every portfolio in the
asset space that incurs no pricing error. In this case, we have no puzzle.
Alternatively, given the SDF space, by dropping some assets from the asset
space we may find a new correctly pricing SDF with sensible parameters
to the reduced asset space. In this way, we can incur no pricing error and
hence there is no puzzle in respect of the smaller asset space. In general,
any mis-matching of an SDF space and an asset space will definitely create
some pricing error. The puzzle can then appear as a result of an improper
attempt to remove the pricing error.

We shall give two examples to illustrate the power of the new structure
theory.

For the first example (2.3.1), the structural theory offers a new explanation of the Mehra and Prescott's puzzle: (1) The structure of the
consumption growth power space is not rich enough to provide an SDF
that is capable of pricing every portfolio in the asset space correctly (*i.e.*,
the two spaces are not isometric), within feasible ranges of the economic
parameters. For example, when the risk aversion is chosen to be less than
5, a big pricing error appears. (2) The structure of the SDF space used is
insufficient so much so that the estimated parameter has to be exaggerated
to an unreasonable level (e.g. beyond 50 for the risk aversion in the U.S.
market) in order to incur no pricing error.

Example 2.3.1 *(The CRRA based SDFs) Here we consider the CRRA-
based SDF family $M_K = \{m = \beta(\frac{c_1}{c_0})^{-\gamma},\ 0 \leq \gamma \leq K,\ 0 < \beta \leq 1\}$ and
assume that there is only one risky asset to be priced. That is $X = \Im_1 =
\{ax\ |\forall a \in \Re\}$. Given market price p for payoff x, a correctly pricing SDF
(also called a pricing kernel) in X is $\hat{a}x$ with $\hat{a} = p/E[x^2]$. Given an m, its
orthogonal projection on X is $T(m) = \hat{E}[m|x] = bx$ with $b = E[mx]/E[x^2]$.
Then m is a correctly pricing SDF if and only $b = a$, and the identity holds
if and only $p = E[mx]$. Define gross return R by $R = x/p$. Then we need
to check*

$$1 = E[mR]. \tag{2.17}$$

*Let g be the consumption growth given by $g = ln(\frac{c_1}{c_0})$. Then $m = \beta e^{-\gamma g}$. It
is conventional to assume that the asset's gross return R and the consump-*

tion growth g are jointly normally distributed, i.e. $(R, g) \sim N(\mu, \Sigma)$, where the mean vector $\mu = (\mu_R, \mu_g)^T$ and the covariance matrix

$$\Sigma = \begin{pmatrix} \sigma_R^2 & \rho \sigma_R \sigma_g \\ \rho \sigma_R \sigma_g & \sigma_g^2 \end{pmatrix}.$$

Here, ρ is the correlation coefficient between R and g, σ_R and σ_g the volatility of R and g respectively, and μ_R and μ_g the mean of R and g respectively. Using the Stein Lemma,

$$E[mR] = cov(e^{-\gamma g}, R) + E[m]E[R]$$

$$= -\gamma \beta E e^{-\gamma g} cov(g, R) + E[m]E[R]$$

$$= (\mu_R - \gamma \rho \sigma_R \sigma_g) E[m]$$

$$= \beta(\mu_R - \gamma \rho \sigma_R \sigma_g) \frac{1}{\sqrt{2\pi}\sigma_g} \int_{-\infty}^{\infty} e^{-\gamma g} e^{-\frac{1}{2}\frac{(g-\mu_g)^2}{\sigma_g^2}} dg \quad (2.18)$$

$$= \beta(\mu_R - \gamma \rho \sigma_R \sigma_g) e^{-\gamma \mu_g + \frac{1}{2}\gamma^2 \sigma_g^2}. \quad (2.19)$$

Therefore we need to look for proper values of the parameters β and γ satisfying

$$1 = \beta(\mu_R - \gamma \rho \sigma_R \sigma_g) e^{-\gamma \mu_g + \frac{1}{2}\gamma^2 \sigma_g^2}. \quad (2.20)$$

Given the consumption data and the market data, it is difficult to obtain an explicit solution for (2.20). Mehra and Prescott (1985) uses the U.S. yearly consumption data and the S&P 500 data from 1889 to 1978 with average consumption growth $\mu_g = 0.76\%$, growth volatility $\sigma_g = 1.54\%$, average S&P500 gross return $\mu_R = 106.98\%$, return's volatility $\sigma_R = 16.54\%$, and correlation between consumption growth and stock return $\rho = 37.56\%$. We see that the average ratio $(\mu_R - 1)/\mu_g = 6.98\%/0.76\% = 9.18$ and the volatility ratio $\sigma_R/\sigma_g = 16.54\%/1.54\% = 10.74$. Mehra and Prescott (op. cit.) has considered many different choices for parameter β. Here we set $\beta = 0.94$ for illustration. By varying γ, we have a plot of the right side of (2.20) as shown in Figure 2.4.

Then we know that when $\gamma = 76.1$, a solution is obtained for (2.20). However, this means that the U.S. investors must be extremely risk averse during the past one hundred years, which is highly unlikely to be the case.

If we use the CRRA-based SDF to price the risky asset x and the risk-free rate R_f, and suppose that m prices risk-free rate correctly, then we

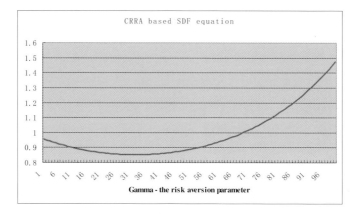

Figure 2.4: Plot of the SDF equation given by the CRRA model.

have $E[m] = 1/R_f$. *Using (2.19), we have a formula for γ namely*

$$\gamma = \frac{\mu_R - R_f}{\sigma_R} \frac{1}{\rho\sigma_g}. \tag{2.21}$$

In Mehra and Prescott's paper, the average gross real return for 90 days U.S. treasury bill is 100.80% and the volatility is 5.67%. Thus the Sharpe ratio $\frac{\mu_R - R_f}{\sigma_R}$ is 0.37. This gives an estimation of γ at 64.6.

In either case, if we consider a small but economically feasible CRRA-based SDF candidate space, M_5 for example, then we will not able to find a correctly pricing SDF for the risky asset - S&P 500. However, if we enlarge the candidate space from M_5 to the bigger space M_{75}, then we will find a correctly pricing SDF, but this creates the so-called Equity Premium Puzzle. We can envisage that if we use the CRRA-based SDF to price more complex asset spaces, larger pricing errors will ensue.

Example (2.3.1) has revealed that in order to find a correctly pricing SDF, we should not exaggerate its parameter space beyond its reasonable range, but rather, given the structure of the asset space, we should enlarge the SDF candidat space by incorporating further appropriate economic state variables.

The next example concerns the Epstein-Zin model. Using the structural theory, we shall see why the model explains the puzzle better. The SDF space generated from the Epstein-Zin model is more complex than the CRRA (constant-relative-risk aversion) based SDF space used by Mehra and Prescott in 1985. In the Epstein-Zin model, the SDF space is spanned by two state variables, namely the consumption growth and the market return. In contrast, the CRRA based SDF space is spanned by only one state variable, namely the single consumption growth. So, within a relatively reasonable range of the parameters, the Epstein-Zin based model is capable of providing a smaller pricing error for the same asset space.

Example 2.3.2 Epstein-Zin utility *Epstein and Zin (1991) introduces a recursive utility by separating the risk aversion parameter γ and the elasticity of inter-temporal substitution parameter δ, namely*

$$U_0 = [(1-\beta)C_0^{1-\delta^{-1}} + \beta[E_0 U_1^{1-\gamma}]^{\frac{1-\delta^{-1}}{1-\gamma}}]^{\frac{1}{1-\delta^{-1}}}. \tag{2.22}$$

It is well known that the Epstein-Zin's SDF has the form

$$m = \beta^{\frac{\delta-\gamma\delta}{\delta-1}} (C_1/C_0)^{-\frac{1-\gamma}{\delta-1}} R^{\frac{1-\delta\gamma}{\delta-1}}, \tag{2.23}$$

where R is the gross market return. Let consumption growth g be $ln(C_1/C_0)$ and stock return $x = ln(R)$. Again we assume that the stock return x and the consumption growth g are jointly normally distributed, i.e. $(x,g) \sim N(\mu, \Sigma)$ as in Example (2.3.1). Then

$$m = \beta_0 e^{-g\lambda_1} e^{x\lambda_2}, \tag{2.24}$$

where $\beta_0 = \beta^{\frac{\delta-\gamma\delta}{\delta-1}}$, $\lambda_1 = \frac{1-\gamma}{\delta-1} xa$ and $\lambda_2 = \frac{1-\delta\gamma}{\delta-1}$. Obviously the Epstein-Zin SDF is spanned by two variables, namely the consumption growth and the market return. Hence the right side of the Euler equation is

$$E[mR] = \beta_0 E[e^{-g\lambda_1} e^{(1+\lambda_2)x}] = \beta_0 E[e^{(1+\lambda_2)x} E[e^{-g\lambda_1}|x]]. \tag{2.25}$$

The conditional distribution of g given x is $N(\mu_{g|x}, \sigma_{g|x})$, where

$$\mu_{g|x} = \mu_g + \rho\frac{\sigma_g}{\sigma_x}(x - \mu_x) \text{ and } \sigma_{g|x}^2 = \sigma_g^2(1-\rho^2). \tag{2.26}$$

In the following, we use the simple result that

$$\int_{-\infty}^{\infty} e^{ax} e^{-\frac{1}{2}\frac{(x-b)^2}{\sigma^2}} dx = \sigma\sqrt{2\pi} e^{ab+\frac{1}{2}a^2\sigma^2},$$

for any two real numbers a and b. We have $E[e^{-g\lambda_1}|x] = e^{x\mu_1+c_1}$, where $\mu_1 = -\lambda_1\rho\frac{\sigma_g}{\sigma_x}$ and $c_1 = -\lambda_1\mu_g + \lambda_1\rho\frac{\sigma_g}{\sigma_x}\mu_x + \frac{1}{2}\lambda_1^2\sigma_g^2(1-\rho^2)$. This gives

$$E[mR] = \beta_0 e^{c_1} E[e^{(1+\lambda_2+\mu_1)x}]$$

$$= \beta_0 e^{c_1 + (1+\lambda_2+\mu_1)\mu_x + \frac{1}{2}(1+\lambda_2+\mu_1)^2\sigma_x^2} \tag{2.27}$$

$$= \beta_0 e^{-\lambda_1\mu_g + \frac{1}{2}\lambda_1^2\sigma_g^2(1-\rho^2) + (1+\lambda_2)\mu_x + \frac{1}{2}(\sigma_x+\lambda_2\sigma_x-\lambda_1\rho\sigma_g)^2}. \tag{2.28}$$

Using the data in Merha and Prescott (1985), we have Figure 2.5 and Table 2.1 for values of $E[mR]$ over various γ and δ. In contrast to the case of the CRRA-based SDF, it is now quite easy to find a risk aversion parameter to satisfy the Euler equation.

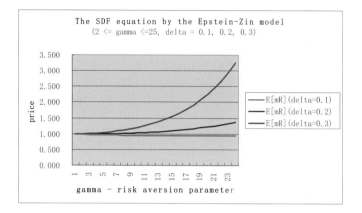

Figure 2.5: Plot of the SDF equation given by the Epstein-Zin model.

Table 2.1: Values of $E[mR]$ given by the Epstein-Zin model ($\beta = 0.95$)

γ	$\delta = 0.1$	$\delta = 0.2$	$\delta = 0.3$
2	0.994	0.996	0.999
3	0.988	0.993	1.003
4	0.983	0.992	1.011
5	0.978	0.992	1.023
6	0.973	0.994	1.040
7	0.969	0.997	1.062
8	0.966	1.002	1.090
9	0.962	1.008	1.122
10	0.959	1.016	1.161

2.4   Conclusions and Summary

In this chapter, we have developed a new theory for asset pricing, which we christen the structural theory. We separate the problem of finding a better asset pricing model from that of searching for no equity premium puzzle. Our first result from the unique theorem and the dual theorem indicates that, given market traded prices, a necessary and sufficient condition for the pricing functional space (or the SDF space) to have a unique *correctly pricing functional* (or *correctly pricing SDF*) is that the space is isometric to the asset space. The orthogonal projection operator, introduced in the dual theorem, provides a bijective and valuation-preserving mapping between the two spaces. The structural theory has provided a new explanation for the Mehra and Prescott puzzle. It indicates that whether there is an equity premium puzzle or not is *relative*, depending on whether or not there is a matching between a SDF space and an asset space. Using the above theory, we have seen why the Epstein-Zin model leads to a more satisfactory resolution.

Chapter 3

Algebra of Stochastic Discount Factors — The Structural Theory of Asset Pricing (Part II)

In this chapter, we develop the structural theory further to deal with an enlarged portfolio space that includes non-tradable assets; we shall discuss asset pricing problems including both the bottom-up investment methodology and the top-down investment methodology. Typical examples of the former include (i) a fund manager first picking some individual stocks and forming a stock portfolio after a series of stock selections, then facing the problem of portfolio valuation based on the individual stocks' valuations and (ii) an U.S. fund manager starting to invest in emerging markets and facing the problem of whether or not he should, either partially or wholly, apply his valuation standard in the U.S. to emerging markets. Typical top-down examples include tactical asset allocations driven by valuation of asset class. Mathematically speaking, these problems become one of pricing problems. Specifically, when investment opportunities increase, which affects the portfolio space (enlarged or reduced), how can a new asset pricing model 'learn' from previous asset pricing models?

3.1 Symmetric Theorem of Asset Pricing with an Application to Value Economic Derivative

Here is the third main result of this book.

Theorem 3.1.1 (Symmetric theorem of correctly pricing functional spaces) *Let H be a claim contingent space as introduced in the last chapter. Let M be an SDF linear closed subspace of H and spanned by some economic variables. Let M^* be the dual space of all continuous linear functionals on M. Then M has a unique correctly pricing SDF for asset space X if and only if M is priced by a unique functional in M^* and M^* is isometric to X, with the understanding that if $X = \bar{\Im}$, Assumption 2.2.1 applies. More precisely, there exists a unique x^{**} in X satisfying*

$$p_i = E[x^{**}m_i], \text{ for } i = 1, 2, \cdots, \tag{3.1}$$

where $\{m_i\}$ is an SDF in M satisfying $\hat{E}[m_i|X] = x_i$ and M is spanned by $\{m_1, \cdots, m_n\}$ if $X = \Im_n$ and by the closure of $\cup_{n=1}^{\infty}\{m_1, \cdots, m_n\}$ in H if $X = \bar{\Im}$.

Proof: For necessity, using the Riesz representation theorem, we know that there is a bijective mapping R_{X^*} from X^* to X. Using Theorem (2.2.4), S is a bijective mapping from X to M. Therefore $S \circ R_{X^*}$ is a bijective mapping from X^* to M. Similarly by using the Riesz representation theorem twice, we have a bijective mapping U from X^{**} to M^* by $U = R_{M^*}^{-1} \circ S \circ R_{X^*} \circ R_{X^{**}}$. Since the Hilbert space X is reflexive, X^{**} is isometric to X by a mapping V. Therefore $W = U \circ V$ is a bijective mapping from X to M^*. Since all Riesz's mappings and S are isometric, we know that mapping W is isometric as well. Let m^0 be the correctly pricing SDF in M and recall that $T = S^{-1}$. Define $x^{**} = T(m^0) \in X$. Then it is easy to see that $p_i = E[m^0 x_i] = E[T(m^0)x_i]$; since $T(m^0) \in X$, then $E[T(m^0)x_i] = E[T(m^0)S(x_i)] = E[T(m^0)m_i] = E[x^{**}m_i]$. That is

$$p_i = E[x^{**}m_i] \text{ for } i = 1, 2, \cdots. \tag{3.2}$$

Now, let us first consider the case when $X = \Im_n$. By Theorem (2.2.4), M has a correctly pricing SDF for X if and only if the mapping S is a continuous linear bijective operator from X to M. Let $m_i = S(x_i)$, $i = 1, 2, \cdots, n$. $\forall m \in M$, using Theorem (2.2.4), $S^{-1}(m) = \hat{E}[m|x] \in X$. Since X is spanned by $\{x_1, \cdots, x_n\}$, we have $\hat{E}[m|X] = \sum_{i=1}^{n} w_i x_i$. Since S is linear, we obtain

$$m = S(\hat{E}[m|x]) = \sum_{i=1}^{n} w_i S(x_i) = \sum_{i=1}^{n} w_i m_i. \tag{3.3}$$

In other words, $M = span\{m_1, \cdots, m_n\}$.

Next, when $X = \bar{\Im}$, let space M_1 be the closure of $\cup_{n=1}^{\infty} span\{m_1, \cdots, m_n\}$. Since for $n \geq 1$, $span\{m_1, \cdots, m_n\} \subset M$ and M is a linear closed subspace in H, we have $M_1 \subset M$. $\forall m \in M$, since $T(m) \in X$, $T(m) = \sum_{i=1}^{\infty} a_i e_i$ with $\sum_{i=1}^{\infty} a_i^2 < \infty$. Define an SDF n_i in M by $n_i = S(e_i)$. Then $m = S(T(m)) = S(\sum_{i=1}^{\infty} a_i e_i) = \sum_{i=1}^{\infty} a_i n_i$. Since each $e_i \in span\{x_1, \cdots, x_i\} = \Im_i$, $n_i = S(e_i) \in span\{m_1, \cdots, m_i\}$. Hence each $n_i \in M_1$. Since M_1 is closed in H, we have $m \in M_1$. Therefore $M \subset M_1$. Putting the two results together, we have $M = M_1$.

For sufficiency, we first note that there is an isometric mapping between X and M^* because of Assumption 2.2.1 and the fact that all Riesz's mappings are isometric. Then the mapping S given by $S = R_{M^*} \circ W \circ V^{-1} \circ R_{X^{**}}^{-1} \circ R_{X^*}^{-1}$ from X to M is isometric. By Theorem (2.2.4), we have completed the proof.

$$Q.E.D.$$

Theorems in the last chapter point out that, given an asset space, we need to find an appropriate economic-factor-driven space that contains a correctly pricing SDF for the asset space. Now, the above symmetric theorem indicates that these economic factors can be traded and priced by a market portfolio, reflexively. Robert Shiller has strongly prompted this idea in his 1993 book entitled *Macro Markets: Creating Institutions for Managing Society's Large Economic Risks*. He proposes to set up macro markets for claims on aggregate income and service flows and other economic risk factors. The symmetric theorem indicates a way to price economic risk factors. See Figure 3.1 for an illustration.

Example 3.1.2 Economic derivatives *Deutsche Bank and Goldman Sachs started in October 2002 to provide vanilla and digital options and range forwards on the U.S. non-farm payroll employment index, the ISM manufacturing index and the U.S. retail sales (ex-autos) index. We refer interested readers to the report in Risk, August 2002 (page 13). Later, ICAP agreed to broker the parimutuel auction-based economic derivatives, including one- and three-month options on the eurozone harmonised index of consumer price (ex-tobacco) inflation index (HICP) and the U.S. consumer price index (CPI) in June, 2003 (see Risk, June 2003, page 13). Barclays Bank also provides options on the Halifax U.K. house price index.*

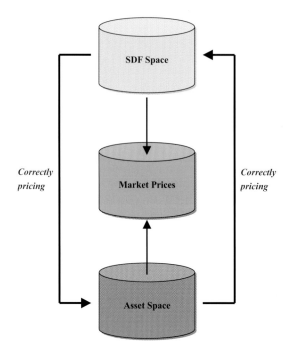

Figure 3.1: Symmetric Theorem between SDF space and asset space.

3.2   Compounding Asset Pricing Models with Applications to Bottom-up Investment Methodology

In the following we consider the problem of compounding two SDFs into one SDF to value a larger asset space. Suppose that we have two asset spaces X_1 and X_2 with SDF spaces M_1 and M_2, and correctly pricing SDFs $m_1 \in M_1$ and $m_2 \in M_2$ for X_1 and X_2, respectively, and we are interested in investing in the combined asset space $X = X_1 + X_2$, where '+' refers to the sum of two sub-linear spaces in a Hilbert space. Financially speaking, it means combining two sub-portfolio spaces to form a large portfolio space. A natural question is whether we can construct a correctly pricing SDF m in $M_1 + M_2$ for $X_1 + X_2$. We notice that $m_1 + m_2$ may not be a correctly pricing SDF for $X_1 + X_2$, though m_1 and m_2 are correctly pricing SDFs for X_1 and X_2 individually. The sources of trouble are as follows: (1) In an enlarged asset space, we may have redundant assets, though both m_1 and m_2 satisfy the parsimoniously pricing condition (2.11) for X_1 and X_2 separately. As an example, consider the case in which $X_1 = span\{x_1, \cdots, x_n\}$ and $X_2 = span\{y_1, \cdots, y_n\}$, but y_2 is represented by a portfolio of $x_1, \cdots, x_n$ plus y_1. Clearly, y_2 is redundant and has to be removed when considering $X_1 + X_2$. (2) Now, m_1 may incur some pricing error for asset space X_2, and m_2 for asset space X_1. Even if we assume that X_1 and X_2 are orthogonal, we still cannot guarantee that m_1 incurs zero pricing error for X_2 and m_2 for X_1. Just consider the extreme case of $M_1 = X_2$ and $M_2 = X_1$. (3) There may exist some common portfolios in X_1 and X_2. Whether or not an arbitrage opportunity exists in the enlarged space depends on how m_1 and m_2 price these common portfolios.

A satisfactory solution of the compounding problem is relevant. For, it will enable us to construct a complex pricing functional from a series of simpler pricing functionals. Further, in practice we do meet the compounding problem frequently. For example, in an international portfolio consisting of some U.S. stocks, say X_{US}, and some U.K. stocks, say X_{UK}. Suppose that we already have correctly pricing domestic SDFs, m_{US} and m_{UK} say, which are functionals of the respective domestic economic variables. The question arises as to how we can price correctly the international portfolio $X_{US} + X_{UK}$, based on information of the U.S. and U.K. economic variables. Put another way, suppose in a global fund management company there are already several highly qualified domestic fund management teams. How can the company develop an efficient global fund management framework by pooling their existing expertise in the US and the UK investments?

Let $V = X_1 \cap X_2$ denote the subspace of common portfolios in X_1 and X_2. It is easy to see that V is a closed subspace. Then we have the orthogonal decompositions of X_1 and X_2:

$$X_1 = V_1 \oplus V \text{ and } X_2 = V \oplus V_2,^1 \qquad (3.4)$$

and

$$X = V_1 + V + V_2. \qquad (3.5)$$

Assumption 3.2.1 Over a common portfolio space say V all SDFs have the same valuation, i.e. for any i and j

$$\hat{E}[m_i|V] = \hat{E}[m_j|V]. \qquad (3.6)$$

---

[1]It is not necessary that V_1 is orthogonal to V_2.

If this assumption does not hold, then an arbitrage opportunity exists. Let us suppose $E[m_1 e_{n+1}] = q_1 \neq q_2 = E[m_2 e_{n+1}]$. If $q_1 < q_2$, then we can take a long position from agent m_1 and a short position from agent m_2, thus obtaining profits with zero-risk. Indeed, in an international portfolio, the HSBC bank is a cross-boundary stock listed in the New York Stock Exchange, the London Stock Exchange and the HongKong Stock Exchange. Given the exchange rates among the U.S. dollar, the H.K. dollar and the sterling and ignoring trading costs, all three markets must give the same valuation to the HSBC bank; otherwise a typical arbitrage opportunity will exist.

Next, we introduce the notion of a *complete SDF pricing space.*

Definition 3.2.1 *Let X be a portfolio space and M be an SDF space that provides pricing candidates to X. Then we say that M is complete to X if it is agreed by all the SDF pricing candidates in M that only assets with zero payoff possess zero price, that is*

$$for \ any \ x \in X, E[mx] = 0, \forall m \in M \Longrightarrow x \equiv 0. \tag{3.7}$$

Lemma 3.2.2 *M is complete to X if and only if the subspace of orthogonal projections of M on X is X itself. That is*

$$\{y = \hat{E}[m|X]; \quad \forall m \in M\} = X. \tag{3.8}$$

Proof: All we need to notice is that $E[mx] = E[\hat{E}[m|X]x]$. By setting $\hat{E}[m|X] = m$, we have our conclusion.

$$\text{Q.E.D.}$$

Here is the fourth main result of this book.

Theorem 3.2.3 (Expanding theorem of correctly pricing functionals) *Given the asset space $X = X_1 + X_2$, let M be the minimum complete expansion of $M_1 + M_2$ to X. Suppose that assumptions (2.1)-(2.2) hold. Then the SDF space M has a unique SDF, denoted by m, that prices portfolio space X correctly. Furthermore, suppose that assumption (3.2.1) holds and V_1 and V_2 are orthogonal. Then the orthogonal projection, $\hat{E}[m|X]$, of m on X is given by*

$$\hat{E}[m|X] = \hat{E}[m_1|X_1] + \hat{E}[m_2|V_2] = \hat{E}[m_1|V_1] + \hat{E}[m_2|X_2]. \tag{3.9}$$

Proof: Let T be the orthogonal projector from M to X. First we check that it is bijective. By the completeness and Lemma (3.2.2), T is surjective. Second, if m and $m' \in M$ with $m \neq m'$ but $T(m) = T(m')$, then for any $x \in X$ with $x \neq 0$, $E[(m - m')x] = E[(T(m) - T(m'))x] = 0$. This contradicts the completeness of M to X. So T must be injective. Hence T is bijective and according to the Dual Theorem, there exists a unique SDF $m \in M$ that prices X correctly. Furthermore, since $\hat{E}[m_1|X] = \hat{E}[m_1|V_1] + \hat{E}[m_1|V] + \hat{E}[m_1|V_2]$ and $\hat{E}[m_2|X] = \hat{E}[m_2|V_1] + \hat{E}[m_2|V] + \hat{E}[m_2|V_2]$, we have

$$\hat{E}[m_1|X_1] + \hat{E}[m_2|V_2] = \hat{E}[m_2|V_2] + \hat{E}[m_1|V_1] + \hat{E}[m_1|V]$$

$$= \hat{E}[m_2|V_2] + \hat{E}[m_1|V_1] + \hat{E}[m_2|V]$$

$$= \hat{E}[m_2|V_2 + V] + \hat{E}[m_1|V_1]$$

$$= \hat{E}[m_2|X_2] + \hat{E}[m_1|V_1].$$

In the above we have used assumption (3.2.1). Thus, we obtain

$$\hat{E}[m_1|X_1] + \hat{E}[m_2|V_2] = \hat{E}[m_1|V_1] + \hat{E}[m_2|X_2]. \tag{3.10}$$

By the uniqueness of orthogonal projection in X, we have

$$T(m) = \hat{E}[m|X] = \hat{E}[m_1|X_1] + \hat{E}[m_2|V_2] = \hat{E}[m_1|V_1] + \hat{E}[m_2|X_2].$$

Q.E.D.

Theorem 3.2.3 highlights several interesting and important aspects of asset pricing.

1. Given a unique correctly pricing SDF m_1 in M_1 to X_1, we have a linear and continuous valuation functional π_1 satisfying $\pi_1(x) = E[m_1 x]$, $\forall x \in X_1$. Similarly we have a linear and continuous valuation functional π_2 for X_2. Then we have an extended functional π, on $X_1 + X_2$, of π_1 and π_2 such that

$$\pi|_{X_1} = \pi_1 \text{ and } \pi|_{X_2} = \pi_2. \tag{3.11}$$

However, when we carry out some practical valuation for $X_1 + X_2$, we have to use an SDF, say m, within some economic contexts to help us make investment decision, since generally π takes only an abstract form. This theorem tells us that we should search a correctly pricing m in a minimum complete expansion, say M, of $M_1 + M_2$ satisfying

$$\pi(x) = E[mx], \ \forall x \in X_1 + X_2, \tag{3.12}$$

because we will not be able to find a correctly pricing SDF in any SDF space strictly smaller than M.

2. Since M_1 has a unique SDF which prices X_1 correctly, the minimum complete expansion of M_1 to X_1 is M_1 itself, according to Lemma 3.2.2. The same applies to the case of M_2 and X_2. However, $M_1 + M_2$ is not necessarily complete. This implies that, though the enlarged portfolio space, $X_1 + X_2$, involves linear combinations of elements of X_1 and X_2, pricing SDF does not simply follow similar linear combinations. For example, suppose M_1 is of dimension n and M_2 is of dimension m. Then we have multi-factor representations such as $m_1 = \sum_{i=1}^{n} a_i f_i$ and $m_2 = \sum_{j=1}^{m} b_j g_j$. In general, we can expect that an element in M is represented by

$$m = \sum_{i=1}^{n} a_i' f_i + \sum_{j=1}^{m} b_j' g_j + \sum_{k} c_k h_k, \tag{3.13}$$

where $\{h_k\}$ are some new pricing factors to do with the covariance structures between X_1 and X_2, M_1 and M_2, M_1 and X_2, and M_2 and X_1.

3. The above theorem reveals the difficulty when using the bottom-up methodology to value a portfolio. We have to deal with new factors $\{h_k\}$ at each upward step. Thus, in building Markowitz's efficient portfolio, each time when we add a new asset into an existing portfolio, we have to re-run the enlarged efficient portfolio. William Sharpe's CAPM model bypasses this difficulty by assuming that there exists a top SDF space or a largest asset space, the so-called market portfolio. And nobody can expand this market portfolio further. All SDFs or rather valuation functionals are only restricted versions of the functional given this market portfolio. In practice, we often use a market index as its proxy or an approximation since we never know what the market portfolio really is.

4. When the whole asset market $\bar{\Im}$ has no-arbitrage, we know that a correctly pricing SDF m_1 to a portfolio X_1 already contains some

"hidden" information about m_2 and X_2. This reflects the fact that valuation is a 'global' matter within a whole asset market while inherent riskiness for each asset is a 'local' matter. The bottom-up strategy exploited by Graham, Buffet and other investors typically acknowledges this. For each individual stock such as the IBM computer company or the BP oil company, analysts first identify its unique risk characteristics such as business models, corporate governance, industrial organization, growths of sale and earning, and so on. In other words, they attempt to build a model of the form

$$X_1 = \sum_i a_i f_i,$$

where the risk factors $\{f_i\}$ include common factors and idiosyncratic factors which are unique to each stock. At this stage, the model has nothing to do with the valuation process but everything to do with the analysts' judgements. Then we need to price fairly X_1 or equivalently $\{f_i\}$, based on all agents' preferences and risk aversions to the whole asset market; otherwise an arbitrage opportunity may appear. Hence, when the SDF pricing equation $p = E[m_i x] \ \forall x \in X_i, \ i = 1, 2$ is used, m_i is not solely determined by the riskiness of X_i. Instead, by going to an even bigger portfolio space X, X_1 and X_2 are priced in X. It just happens that m_1's 'pricing agents' do not know m_2's, and vice versa.

5. In practice, when asset markets X_1 and X_2 are not connected, as is the case with the current situation between the Chinese stock market and the U.S. stock market, investors in the two markets have developed their respective correctly pricing SDFs. However, the moment when the two markets become connected, there are typically some initial but limited arbitrage opportunities. In this situation, either m_1 or m_2 or both begin to change until the two markets reach a no-arbitrage state. Meanwhile fundamental risks of the Chinese stocks and the U.S. stocks are still there and unchanged.

See Figure 3.2 for an illustration.

Corollary 3.2.4 Expanding theorem of correctly pricing functionals in a very special case. *Suppose that assumptions (2.2.1)- (3.2.1) hold and X has no redundant assets. If asset spaces $X_1 = span\{x_1, \cdots, x_n\}$ and $X_2 = span\{y_1, \cdots, y_k\}$, m_1 is the correctly pricing SDF for X_1, satisfying*

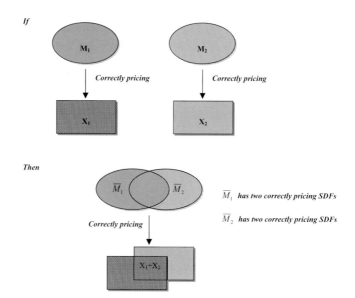

Figure 3.2: Expanding Theorem for SDF spaces and asset spaces.

$p_i = E[m_1 x_i]$, $i = 1, \cdots, n$, and m_2 is the correctly pricing SDF for X_2, satisfying $q_j = E[m_2 y_j]$, $j = 1, \cdots, k$, then the SDF above satisfies $m \in M$ and

$$p_i = E[m x_i], \ i = 1, \cdots, n \text{ and } q_j = E[m y_j], \ j = 1, \cdots, k. \quad (3.14)$$

In particular, if $n = k = 1$ and $d = [p_1 q_1 - < m_2, x_1 >< m_1, y_1 >] \neq 0$, then

$$m = w_1 m_1 + w_2 m_2,^2 \quad (3.15)$$

where $w_1 = \frac{1}{d}[p_1 - < m_2, x_1 >] q_1$ and $w_2 = \frac{1}{d}[q_1 - < m_1, y_1 >] p_1$, is a correctly pricing SDF.

Proof: From the proof of Theorem (3.2.3), it is easy to have pricing equation (3.14). To prove pricing equation (3.15), we can solve for w_1 and w_2 in two equations: $p_1 =< m, x_1 >$ and $q_1 =< m, y_1 >$. We have $p_1 =< m, x_1 >= w_1 < m_1, x_1 > + w_2 < m_2, x_1 >$ and $q_1 = w_1 < m_1, y_1 > + w_2 < m_2, y_1 >$, which give $w_1 = \frac{1}{d}[p_1 - < m_2, x_1 >] q_1$ and $w_2 = \frac{1}{d}[q_1 - < m_1, y_1 >] p_1$.

Q.E.D.

---

[2]If $n > 1$ or $k > 1$, formula (3.15) cannot provide a correctly pricing SDF for X.

Example 3.2.5 International index portfolio *Suppose that $x_1 =$ the U.S. S&P 500 index and $x_2 =$ the U.K. FTSE 100 index. Suppose that $SDF_{S\&P500index}$ is the correctly pricing SDF for the U.S. S&P 500 index tracking fund. Similarly suppose that $SDF_{FTSE100index}$ is the correctly pricing SDF for the U.K. FTSE 100 index tracking fund. Then in order to have correctly pricing for the international index portfolio consisting of x_1, x_2, we have to generate a proper SDF from the two-dimensional SDF space $(SDF_{S\&P500index}, SDF_{FTSE100index})$ by $SDF = w_1 SDF_{S\&P500index} + w_2 SDF_{FTSE100index}$.*

3.3 Compression of Asset Pricing Models with Applications to Top-down Investment Methodology

Since we have argued that valuation of a portfolio is a matter related to itself, we face a complexity problem due to the number of assets. For example, in the U.S. market, there are thousands of stocks; if we want to do an index valuation such as Russell 3000 small-cap index, it is infeasible to value 3000 stocks one by one. We need some method of compression. In the top-down pricing methodology, all assets are priced by their finitely many common risk factors; the assets have zero valuation for their own idiosyncratic risk factor. (The bottom-up valuation methodology, such as Buffet's value strategy, assigns non-zero valuation to idiosyncratic risk factors.) Based on the Law of Large Number, Ross's APT (1976) develops a compression method for asset pricing by pricing the common factors. Chamberlain and Rothschild(1983) and Chamberlain (1983) have built the APT involving large number of assets. In the following, we will develop a top-down correctly pricing methodology.

Definition 3.3.1 *Let x_f be an element in $\bar{\Im}$. Then $x_f \neq 0$ is called a riskless limit portfolio if $V(x_f) = 0$ and $E[x_f] \neq 0$. Let $R_f = x_f / E[x_f] \in \bar{\Im}$. Then R_f is called a riskless asset.*

Lemma 3.3.2 *If $\bar{\Im}$ has no riskless limit portfolio, then $\bar{\Im}$ is a Hilbert space under the covariance inner product, that is, $\forall x, y \in \bar{\Im}$, we can define $< x, y >= cov(x, y)$, where $cov(x, y)$ is the covariance between x and y.*

Proof: If $< x, x >= cov(x, x) = V(x) = 0$, then we have $x = E[x]$ in H. If $E[x] \neq 0$, then $\bar{\Im}$ has a riskless limit portfolio. This is a contradiction.

Therefore we must have $E[x] = 0$ so that $x = 0$. We can easily verify that other properties for an inner product are satisfied with the exception of the completeness of $\bar{\Im}$ under the covariance as an inner product. Suppose there is a sequence $\{x^n\}$ in $\bar{\Im}$ satisfying $< x^n - x^m, x^n - x^m > \to 0$ as n and $m \to \infty$. Since $< x^n - x^m, x^n - x^m > = Cov(x^n - x^m, x^n - x^m) = E(x^n - x^m)^2 + (Ex^n - Ex^m)^2$, then $||x^n - x^m||^2 = E(x^n - x^m)^2 \to 0$. Since $\bar{\Im}$ is complete under the norm $||.||$, there is $x \in \bar{\Im}$ satisfying $||x^n - x|| \to 0$. By the Cauchy-Schwartz Inequality, $(Ex^n - Ex)^2 \leq E[x^n - x]^2 = ||x^n - x||^2$. Hence $V(x^n - x) \to 0$. This means that $\bar{\Im}$ is complete under the covariance as an inner product and $\bar{\Im}$ is a Hilbert space correspondingly.

$$Q.E.D.$$

Suppose $\bar{\Im}$ has a riskless limit portfolio, say x_f. Define excess payoffs by $z_i = x_i - \mu_i R_f$, $i = 1, 2, \cdots$, where $\mu_i = E[x_i]$. Define linear spaces $\Psi_n = span\{z_1, \cdots, z_n\}$, $\Psi = \cup_{n=1}^{\infty} \Psi_n$ and $\bar{\Psi}$ as the closure of Ψ. For each $i = 1, 2, \cdots$, $E[z_i] = E[x_i] - \mu_i E[R_f] = 0$. It is easy to see that $\bar{\Psi}$ has no riskless limit portfolio and hence the covariance can be regarded as an inner product for $\bar{\Psi}$. Therefore $\bar{\Psi}$ is a Hilbert space and a closed linear space of $\bar{\Im}$.

Define $\bar{\Im}_1 = \bar{\Im}$ if $\bar{\Im}$ has no riskless limit portfolio and $\bar{\Im}_1 = \bar{\Psi}$ otherwise.

Definition 3.3.3 *By a well-diversified portfolio space, we mean the space* $D = \{x \in \bar{\Im}_1|$ *there exists a sequence of* $x^n = \sum_{i=1}^{n} a_{i,n} z_i$ *with* $x^n \to x$, $\sum_{i=1}^{n} a_{i,n}^2 \to 0$ *as* $n \to \infty\}$, *where* $z_i = x_i - \mu_i R_f$, $i = 1, 2, \cdots$, *if* $\bar{\Im}$ *has a riskless limit portfolio, and* $z_i = x_i, i = 1, 2, \cdots$, *if* $\bar{\Im}$ *has no riskless limit portfolio.*

According to the Ross Arbitrage Pricing Theory, a well-diversified portfolio should only incur factor risk but no idiosyncratic risk. Normally there exist only finitely many risk factors. Here we introduce the following definition.

Definition 3.3.4 *We say that the asset space* $\bar{\Im}_1$ *has a K-factor structure if* $dim(D) = K < \infty$.

This means that if the well-diversified portfolio space D has dimension K, then D is spanned by only K orthonormal basis elements $\{f_1, \cdots, f_K\}$ satisfying

$$cov(f_i, f_j) = 0 \text{ if } i \neq j \text{ and } V(f_i) = 1, \ i, j = 1, \cdots, K. \qquad (3.16)$$

The payoffs are represented by

$$z_i = \beta_{i,1}f_1 + \cdots + \beta_{i,K}f_K + \epsilon_i, \text{ for } i = 1, 2, \cdots, \qquad (3.17)$$

where factor loadings $\beta_{i,k} = cov(z_i, f_k)$ and $cov(\epsilon_i, f_k) = 0$ for $k = 1, \cdots K$. In particular if $\bar{\Im}$ has no riskless limit portfolio, then

$$x_i = \mu_i + \beta_{i,1}f_1' + \cdots + \beta_{i,K}f_K' + \epsilon_i' \text{ for } i = 1, 2, \cdots, \qquad (3.18)$$

where $\mu_i = E[x_i]$, $f_k' = f_k - E[f_k]$ and $\epsilon_i' = \epsilon_i - E[\epsilon_i]$. If $\bar{\Im}$ has a riskless limit portfolio, then

$$x_i = \mu_i R_f + \beta_{i,1}f_1 + \cdots + \beta_{i,K}f_K + \epsilon_i \text{ for } i = 1, 2, \cdots \qquad (3.19)$$

with $E[f_k] = 0$ and $E[\epsilon_i] = 0$.

Let $\epsilon^n = (\epsilon_1, \cdots, \epsilon_n)$ and the second-moment matrix $S_\epsilon^n = E[\epsilon^n(\epsilon^n)^T]$ of ϵ^n. Let λ_{max}^n be the largest eigenvalue of S_ϵ^n. To have diminishing idiosyncratic risk, we have to make the following assumption.

Assumption 3.3.1 $\lambda = \max_{n \geq 1}\{\lambda_{max}^n\} < \infty$.

Here is the fifth main result of this book.

Theorem 3.3.5 (Compression theorem of correctly pricing functionals) *Suppose that Assumptions 2.1.1, 2.2.1 and 3.3.1 hold. Let $\bar{\Im}_1^*$ be the dual space of $\bar{\Im}_1$. Suppose that F is a linear subspace of $\bar{\Im}_1^*$ and has a unique correctly pricing functional on $\bar{\Im}_1$. Then $\bar{\Im}_1$ has a K-factor structure if and only if F has a K-factor structure as well. That is $F = D^* + (D^*)^\perp$, and D^* is well diversified with K-factor structure. $\forall \pi \in F$, $\pi = \sum_{k=1}^K b_k f_k^* + \epsilon^*$, where $b_k = <\pi, f_k^*>$, the pricing functionals $\{f_k^*\} \subset D^*$ satisfy $< f_k^*, f_j^* >= 0$ for $k \neq j$,$< f_k^*, f_k^* >= 1$ and $< f_k^*, \epsilon^* >= 0$ for $k = 1, \cdots, K$, and $\epsilon^* \in (D^*)^\perp$. A similar conclusion applies to an SDF space.[3]*

Proof: To prove necessity, suppose $\bar{\Im}_1 = \bar{\Im}$ (*i.e.* no riskless limit portfolio). Define pricing functional π_i by $\forall x \in \bar{\Im}$, $\pi_i(x) = E[x_i x]$. Then we define a space $D^* = \{\pi \in \bar{\Im}^* |$ there exists a sequence of pricing functionals $\pi^n = \sum_{i=1}^n a_{i,n}\pi_i$ with $\pi^n \to \pi, \sum_{i=1}^n a_{i,n}^2 \to 0$ as $n \to \infty\}$. Since F has one correctly pricing functional, by Theorem 2.1, $F = \bar{\Im}^*$. Then we know that D^* is a linear subspace of F. Since $\bar{\Im}_1$ has a K-factor structure, there is

---

[3]Cochrane (2000) has used this result without giving a rigorous proof.

an orthogonal decomposition $\bar{\Im}_1 = D + D^\perp$. For all $y \in D^\perp$ and $\pi^n \in D^*$, $\pi^n(y) = \sum_{i=1}^n a_{i,n}\pi_i(y) = \sum_{i=1}^n a_{i,n}E[x_iy] = E[(\sum_{i=1}^n a_{i,n}\epsilon_i)y]$. Hence, by the Cauchy-Schwartz inequality,

$$|\pi^n(y)| = |E[(\sum_{i=1}^n a_{i,n}\epsilon_i)y]| \le \{(a^n)^T S_\epsilon^n a^n\}^{\frac{1}{2}}\{E[y^2]\}^{\frac{1}{2}},$$

where S_ϵ is the covariance matrix of $\epsilon^n = (\epsilon_1, \cdots, \epsilon_n)^T$ and $a^n = (a_{1,n}, \cdots, a_{n,n})^T$. By the singular-value decomposition, we have $S_\epsilon^n = U\Pi U^T$, where U is an orthogonal matrix with $UU^T = I$ and Π is a diagonal matrix $\Pi = diag(\lambda_1, \cdots, \lambda_n)$ with eigenvalues $\{\lambda_i\}$. Using Assumption (3.3.1), we have $|\pi^n(y)| \le \lambda\{E[y^2]\}^{\frac{1}{2}}(\sum_{i=1}^n a_{i,n}^2)$. Letting $n \to \infty$, for $\forall \pi \in D^*$, we have $\pi(y) = \lim_{n\to\infty}\pi^n(y) = 0$. By the Riesz Representation Theorem, for pricing functional π, there is an $x_\pi \in \bar{\Im}_1$ satisfying $\forall x \in \bar{\Im}_1$, $\pi(x) = E[x_\pi x]$. Since $\pi(y) = 0$ for all $y \in D^\perp$, we have $x_\pi \in D$. According to Definition (3.3.4), D has dimension K and is spanned by $f_1, \cdots, f_K$. We have $x_\pi = b_1 f_1 + \cdots + b_K f_K$. Define pricing functional f_k^* by $\forall x \in \bar{\Im}_1$, $f_k^*(x) = E[f_k x]$. Then it is easy to see $< f_k^*, f_j^* > = 0$ if $k \ne j$ and D^* is spanned by $f_1^*, \cdots, f_K^*$ ($\forall \pi \in D^*$, $\pi = b_1 f_1^* + \cdots + b_K f_K^*$.) Therefore pricing functional subspace F has a K-factor structure D^*. The same treatment applies to $\bar{\Im}_1 = \bar{\Psi}$ (*i.e.* there is a riskless limit portfolio). Also the above argument applies to an SDF space.

To prove sufficiency, note that using Theorem (3.1.1), we can regard asset space $\bar{\Im}_1$ as a correctly pricing SDF space for the dual space $\bar{\Im}_1^*$, and then apply the necessary condition to the 'virtual SDF pricing' space $\bar{\Im}_1$.

Q.E.D.

The implication of Theorem (3.3.5) is that if the payoffs of assets are either correlated with or not hedged against risk factors (such as the growth of consumption, the GDP, the inflation, the interest rate, the monetary and fiscal policies, the business cycle, the average earning growth of stocks and so on), then in order to obtain a correctly pricing functional, or SDF, the candidate space must be spanned by the above stated economic factors, or their equivalents under valuation-preserving isometry. For example, using the CRRA model and insisting that it has provided correctly pricing imply the assumption that the asset market has a one-factor structure, and using the Epstein and Zin's model implies the assumption that the asset market has a two-factor structure. In fact, even the asset market has a one-factor structure. For example, suppose that the asset market follows the CAPM

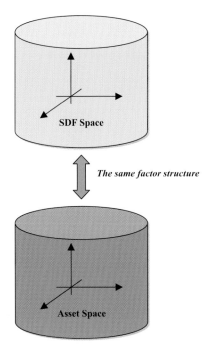

Figure 3.3: Compression Theorem for SDF spaces and asset spaces.

model, then the single factor is the market return and not consumption growth. In order to have correctly pricing to the asset market driven by the market return, we need to have zero effects of means, variances and correlations in equation (3.25) (to be given later) between the market return and the consumption growth. However, when the asset market is not complete, it is hard to have such a perfect match between the market return and the consumption growth. In this case, a pricing error can appear.

See Figure 3.3 for an illustration.

Example 3.3.6 Fama-French's three factor *In Fama and French (1992) and a series of subsequent papers by the same authors, they build a three-factor model*

$$E[R] - R_f = \beta(E[R_m] - R_f) + \beta_{SMB}SMB + \beta_{HML}HML. \quad (3.20)$$

If the stock market is spanned by these three factors, then according to the compression theorem, the SDF space must be spanned by a three-factor structure as well. For example, besides consumption, we should also consider unemployment, inflation, monetary and fiscal policies, technological progress, human capital economic variables and so on.

Corollary 3.3.7 *Suppose that payoffs $\{x_i\} \subset D$, i.e. $\{x_i\}$ are well diversified. If pricing functional π is the correctly pricing functional for $\{x_i\}$, then $\pi \in D^*$. In other words, π is a well diversified pricing functional in $\Im_1^*$ as well.*

3.4   Decomposition of Errors in Asset Pricing Models

Given market prices $\{p_1, \cdots, p_n\}$, Hansen and Jagannathan (1997) introduces a space of correctly pricing functionals by

$$M = \{\pi \in H^* \mid p_i = \pi(x_i), \ i = 1, \cdots, n\} \tag{3.21}$$

$$= \{m \in H \mid p_i = E[mx_i], \ i = 1, \cdots, n\}.$$

Then M is a convex subspace but not a linear subspace of H. Let π be a correctly pricing functional and $\hat{\pi}$ be a continuous pricing functional. Hansen and Jagannathan (*op.cit.*) defines a maximum pricing error by

$$d = sup\{|\hat{\pi}(x) - \pi(x)| \text{ over } x \in \Im_n, \ ||x|| = 1\}. \tag{3.22}$$

Theorem 3.4.1 Pricing error theorem. *Let m be an unknown correctly pricing SDF for asset space $\Im_n$. Let $\hat{m}$ be an SDF proxy that often is a nonlinear function of several economic variables. Then the pricing error due to $\hat{m}$ is given by d, which may be expressed as follows:*

1.

$$d = || \hat{E}[\hat{m}|\Im_n] - \hat{E}[m|\Im_n] || \tag{3.23}$$

$$= [(E[\hat{E}[\hat{m}|\Im_n]] - E[\hat{E}[m|\Im_n]])^2$$

$$+ (1 + \lambda^2)\sigma^2_{\hat{E}[m|\Im_n]} - 2\rho\lambda\sigma^2_{\hat{E}[m|\Im_n]}]^{\frac{1}{2}} \tag{3.24}$$

$$= [d_{mean} + d_{variance} + d_{correlation}]^{\frac{1}{2}}, \tag{3.25}$$

where $\hat{E}[\hat{m}|\Im_n]$ and $\hat{E}[m|\Im_n]$ are the orthogonal projections of $\hat{m}$ and m on $\Im_n$ respectively, ρ is the correlation coefficient between $\hat{E}[\hat{m}|\Im_n]$ and $\hat{E}[m|\Im_n]$, and λ is volatility ratio given by $\lambda = \frac{\sigma_{\hat{E}[\hat{m}|\Im_n]}}{\sigma_{\hat{E}[m|\Im_n]}}$.

In other words, the pricing error comes from three parts: (a) d_{mean}, the difference in means of the orthogonal projections, which measures the pricing error of the inverses of riskless asset R_f by m and $\hat{m}$; (b) $d_{variance}$, which measures the deviation of the variance $\sigma^2_{\hat{E}[\hat{m}|\Im_n]}$ from the variance $\sigma^2_{\hat{E}[m|\Im_n]}$; [Ideally, given the correlation $\rho > 0$, then the optimal variance ratio $\lambda = \rho$, and a minimum pricing error is $d = \sqrt{d_{mean} + (1 - \rho^2)\sigma^2_{\hat{E}[m|\Im_n]}}$]. (c) $d_{correlation}$, which measures the contribution of the pricing error from any correlation between $\hat{E}[\hat{m}|\Im_n]$ and $\hat{E}[m|\Im_n]$. [Ideally, $\rho = 1$].

2. *Suppose that $\hat{E}[m|\Im_n] = \sum_{i=1}^{n} a_i e_i$ and, without loss of generality, we assume that $\hat{E}[\hat{m}|\Im_n] \in \Im_L$, where $\Im_L$ is the subspace of $\Im_n$ with $L \leq n$, and a representation $\hat{E}[\hat{m}|\Im_n] = \sum_{i=1}^{L} b_i e_i$. Then we have*

$$d = \sqrt{\sum_{i=1}^{L}(a_i - b_i)^2 + \sum_{i=L+1}^{n} a_i^2} > 0. \qquad (3.26)$$

3. *Equivalently if we represent $\hat{E}[m|\Im_n]$ and $\hat{E}[\hat{m}|\Im_n]$ by $\hat{E}[m|\Im_n] = \sum_{i=1}^{n} w_i x_i$ and $\hat{E}[\hat{m}|\Im_n] = \sum_{i=1}^{n} v_i x_i$ respectively, where $v_i = 0$ for $i > L$, then we have the well-known Hansen-Jagannathan distance*

$$d = \sqrt{(w - v)^T S_n (w - v)} \qquad (3.27)$$

$$= \sqrt{(p^n - E[\hat{m}x^n])^T S_n^{-1}(p^n - E[\hat{m}x^n])}, \qquad (3.28)$$

where S_n is the second moment of the payoff vector $x^n = (x_1, \cdots, x_n)^T$, i.e. $S_n = E[x^n(x^n)^T]$.

4. *If we further assume that $E[\hat{E}[\hat{m}|\Im_n]] = E[\hat{E}[m|\Im_n]]$, then*

$$d = \sqrt{(w - v)^T \Sigma_n (w - v)}, \qquad (3.29)$$

where the weight vectors $w = (w_1, \cdots, w_n)^T$ and $v = (v_1, \cdots, v_n)^T$.

Proof: The main ideas of the proof come from Hansen and Jagannathan (1997). Since $\forall x \in \Im_n$, $\pi(x) = E[mx] = E[\hat{E}[m|\Im_n]x]$. Without loss of generality, we can assume that $\hat{m}$ and $m \in \Im_n$. $\forall x \in \Im_n$ with $\|x\| = 1$, by the Cauchy-Schwartz inequality, $|\hat{\pi}(x) - \pi(x)| = |E[(\hat{m} - m)x]| \leq \{E[\hat{m} - m]^2\}^{\frac{1}{2}}\{E[x]^2\}^{\frac{1}{2}} = \|\hat{m} - m\|$. Hence $d \leq \|\hat{m} - m\|$. On the other hand, since $||\hat{m} - m|| > 0$ (otherwise we have simply $\hat{m} = m$ and $d = 0$), define payoff $\tilde{m} = (m - \hat{m})/||m - \hat{m}||$. We have $\pi(\tilde{m}) - \hat{\pi}(\tilde{m}) = E[m\tilde{m}] - E[\hat{m}\tilde{m}] = E[(m - \hat{m})\tilde{m}] = E[m - \hat{m}]^2/||m - \hat{m}|| = ||m - \hat{m}||$. Since $||\tilde{m}|| = 1$, $d \geq \pi(\tilde{m}) - \hat{\pi}(\tilde{m}) = ||m - \hat{m}||$. Therefore we have proved that $d = || \hat{E}[\hat{m}|\Im_n] - \hat{E}[m|\Im_n] ||$. By using $E[\xi - \eta]^2 = (E[\xi] - E[\eta])^2 + cov(\xi - \eta, \xi - \eta) = (E[\xi] - E[\eta])^2 + \sigma_\xi^2 + \sigma_\eta^2 - 2\rho\sigma_\xi\sigma_\eta$ for any two random variables ξ and η, we obtain the pricing error decomposition formulas (3.24) and (3.25). Using (3.23), (3.26) and (3.27) can be calculated easily. To show (3.28), since $m|_{\Im_n}$ is an orthogonal projection of m on $\Im_n$, we have

$$v = S_n^{-1} E[\hat{m}x^n]. \qquad (3.30)$$

Next, since m is a correctly pricing SDF, we have $p_i = E[mx_i] = \sum_{j=1}^{n} w_j E[x_i x_j]$ for $i = 1, \cdots, n$. Hence we obtain an 'exact' estimation of $w = (w_1, \cdots, w_n)$ by

$$w = S_n^{-1} p^n . \qquad (3.31)$$

Therefore,

$$d = \sqrt{(w - v)^T S_n (w - v)} = \sqrt{(p^n - E[\hat{m}x^n])^T S_n^{-1} S_n S_n^{-1} (p^n - E[\hat{m}x^n])}$$

$$= \sqrt{(p^n - E[\hat{m}x^n])^T S_n^{-1} (p^n - E[\hat{m}x^n])}.$$

Q.E.D.

From (3.26), we see that a pricing error can come from two sources: (1) the most serious is due to the mistake of searching correctly pricing functional in an insufficient candidate space, which gives a strictly positive pricing error $\sum_{i=L+1}^{n} a_i^2 > 0$; (2) even if we search in a proper space (*i.e.* $L = n$), we can still incur non-negative pricing error $\sum_{i=1}^{L} (a_i - b_i)^2 \geq 0$, due to wrong parameter estimation.

See Figures 3.4 and 3.5 for illustrations.

Furthermore we have an exact decomposition of pricing error over each asset.

Corollary 3.4.2 *Define the representation error between m and $\hat{m}$ by the coefficient vector $w - v$. Then there is no pricing error ($\hat{E}[\hat{m}|\Im_n] = \hat{E}[m|\Im_n]$) if and only if $w - v = 0$. In general, we have a decomposition of the representation error vector $w - v$ by*

$$w - v = \sigma_m \Sigma_n^{-1} b_{corr} + (\sigma_m - \sigma_{\hat{m}}) \Sigma_n^{-1} \sigma = I_\rho + I_\sigma, ^4 \qquad (3.32)$$

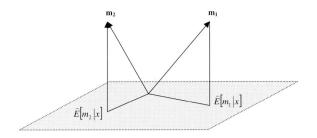

Then to check two random variables

$$U_1 = \widehat{E}\big[m_1\,|\,x\big]$$

And $U_2 = \widehat{E}\big[m_2\,|\,x\big]$

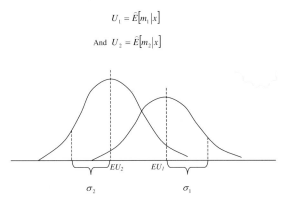

Namely to compare

(1) $EU_1 \overset{?}{=} EU_2$

(2) $\sigma_1 \overset{?}{=} \sigma_2$

Figure 3.4: Pricing Error Theorem.

where the vector of differences of correlations $b_{corr} = ((\rho_{m,x_1} - \rho_{\hat{m},x_1})\sigma_1, \cdots, (\rho_{m,x_n} - \rho_{\hat{m},x_n})\sigma_n)^T$, ρ_{m,x_i} is the correlation coefficient between m and x_i, $\rho_{\hat{m},x_i}$ is the correlation coefficient between $\hat{m}$ and x_i, σ_m is the volatility of m, $\sigma_{\hat{m}}$ is the volatility of $\hat{m}$, and $\sigma = (\sigma_1\rho_{\hat{m},x_1}, \cdots, \sigma_n\rho_{\hat{m},x_n})$ is the weighted volatility vector of payoffs. I_ρ is the error vector due to the difference between the correlation of m and payoffs $\{x_i\}$ and the correlation of $\hat{m}$ and payoffs $\{x_i\}$. I_σ is the error vector due to the difference between the volatility of m and the volatility of $\hat{m}$.

---

[4]When the equity premium puzzle is referred to, the main concern tends to be with SDF's I_σ volatility difference and with the I_ρ correlation difference being typically ignored.

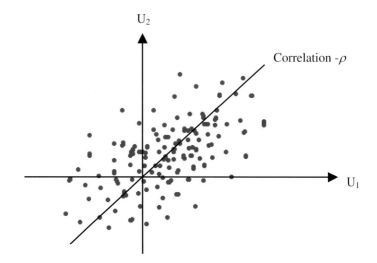

Figure 3.5: Comparing correlation error in the Pricing Error Theorem.

Proof: It is straightforward to see that $\hat{E}[\hat{m}|\Im_n] = \hat{E}[m|\Im_n]$ if and only if $w - v = 0$. Without loss of generality, we can assume that $m,\ \hat{m} \in \Im_n$. Since $m = \sum_{j=1}^{n} w_j x_j$, we have $m - E(m) = \sum_{j=1}^{n} w_j (x_j - E[x_j])$. Multiplying both sides of the equation by $(x_i - E[x_i])$ and taking expectation, we obtain

$$Cov(m, x_i) = E[(m - E[m])(x_i - E[x_i])]$$

$$= \sum_{j=1}^{n} w_j Cov(x_i, x_j). \qquad (3.33)$$

Hence we have $w = \Sigma_n^{-1} Cov(m, x)$, where Σ_n is the covariance matrix of $x = (x_1, \cdots, x_n)^T$ and $Cov(m, x)$ is the covariance vector $(Cov(m, x_1), \cdots, Cov(m, x_n))^T$. Similarly we have $v = \Sigma_n^{-1} Cov(\hat{m}, x)$. Hence $w - v = \Sigma_n^{-1}(Cov(m, x) - Cov(\hat{m}, x))$. Because $Cov(m, x_i) - Cov(\hat{m}, x_i) = (\rho_{m,x_i} - \rho_{\hat{m},x_i})\sigma_m \sigma_i + (\sigma_m - \sigma_{\hat{m}})\sigma_i \rho_{\hat{m},x_i}$, therefore $Cov(m, x) - Cov(\hat{m}, x) = \sigma_m b_{corr} + (\sigma_m - \sigma_{\hat{m}}))\sigma$. We have completed the proof of the corollary.

Q.E.D.

3.5 Empirical Analysis of the Asset Pricing Models

3.5.1 The data set and utility forms

The data sets we use here are the quarterly real returns of S&P 500 index and the one-month U.S. treasury bill over the period from the first quarter of 1950 to the last quarter of 2002. The U.S. real per capita consumption data are extracted from the nominal consumption data adjusted by the CPI data over the same period. Stock data are the quarterly real returns of the American Electric Power Co. Inc. (AEP), the General Electric Co. (GE), the General Motors Corp. (GM), the International Business Machines Corp. (IBM) and the Exxon Mobil Corp. (XOM), over the period from the first quarter of 1970 to the last quarter of 2002.[5] The companies are components of the Dow Jones industrial average index.

Let m_0 be a correct but unknown pricing SDF for the asset space $\Im_n = span\{x_1, \cdots x_n\}$. Let m be the orthogonal projection of m_0 on $\Im_n$, *i.e.* $m = \hat{E}[m_0|\Im_n]$ and takes the form

$$m = \mathbf{c}' \cdot \mathbf{x}, \tag{3.34}$$

where $\mathbf{c}$ is a parameter vector, $\mathbf{x}$ is the payoff vector of asset $\mathbf{x} = \{x_1, \cdots x_n\}$. The parameters can be estimated using the least squares method.

Let $\hat{m}$ be an SDF which may be taken as a proxy for m_0. Suppose that $\hat{m}$ has one of the following forms:

- CRRA utility

$$\hat{m}_{t+1} = \beta \left(\frac{c_{t+1}}{c_t} \right)^{-\gamma}, \tag{3.35}$$

  where β is a subjective discount factor, $0 < \beta < 1$, γ is the coefficient of relative risk aversion, c is the consumption.

- Abel utility

$$\hat{m}_{t+1} = \beta \left(\frac{c_{t+1}}{c_t} \right)^{-\gamma} \left(\frac{c_t}{c_{t-1}} \right)^{\gamma-1}, \tag{3.36}$$

  where γ is the coefficient of relative risk aversion.

---

[5]The quarterly real returns of S&P 500 index are taken from Robert Shiller's homepage. The quarterly returns of the one-month treasury bill come from the Federal Reserve Bank. The per capita consumption and the CPI data are taken from the Bureau of Economic Analysis (BEA). The data for the five listed companies come from the Yahoo finance website.

- Constantindes utility

$$\hat{m}_{t+1} = \beta \left(\frac{c_{t+1}}{c_t} \right)^{-\gamma} \left(\frac{1 - h_{t+1}/c_{t+1}}{1 - h_t/c_t} \right)^{-\gamma}, \qquad (3.37)$$

where $h_t = \varphi c_{t-1}$, γ and φ are parameters.

- Epstein-Zin utility

$$\hat{m}_{t+1} = \beta^{\frac{\eta - \eta\gamma}{\eta - 1}} \left(\frac{c_{t+1}}{c_t} \right)^{-\frac{1-\gamma}{\eta-1}} R_{m,t+1}^{\frac{1-\eta\gamma}{\eta-1}}, \qquad (3.38)$$

where η is the elasticity of intertemporal substitution, γ is the coefficient of relative risk aversion and R_m is the gross return of the market portfolio.

3.5.2   Three sources of pricing errors

Part 1 of Theorem (3.4.1) indicates that the pricing error d consists of three parts, namely the differences in the means, the differences in the volatilities and the imperfect correlation. From Tables 3.1-3.5, we can see that the difference in the means given by the orthogonal projections of two SDFs is very small over various parameters. The CRRA-type pricing model provides the worst scenario among all candidate SDFs. It provides smaller volatility and even negative correlation. The negativeness is very stable over different risk aversion parameters. This indicates that a wrong SDF has been chosen, if we accept that over the past 100 years the historical equity premium has been correct. However, by varying risk aversions, the volatility ratio is improved impressively. The Abel model and the Constantindes model provide a similar pattern of correlation and volatility ratio, but a slightly better result than the CRRA model. Not surprisingly, since the Epstein-Zin model is spanned by two state variables and is more complex

Table 3.1:   Three sources of pricing errors in the CRRA model ($\beta = 0.95$)

γ	d_{mean}	ρ	λ
5	0.0018	-0.66	0.011
15	0.0074	-0.66	0.031
30	0.0208	-0.66	0.056

Table 3.2: Three sources of pricing errors in the Abel model ($\beta = 0.95$)

γ	d_{mean}	ρ	λ
5	0.0005	-0.69	0.018
15	0.0004	-0.69	0.057
30	0.0000	-0.68	0.114

Table 3.3: Three sources of pricing errors in the Constantinides model ($\beta = 0.95, \gamma = 5$)

θ	d_{mean}	ρ	λ
0.1	0.0018	-0.66	0.013
0.5	0.0017	-0.68	0.031
0.9	0.0000	-0.66	0.169

Table 3.4: Three sources of pricing errors in the Epstein-Zin model ($\beta = 0.95, \gamma = 5$)

η	d_{mean}	ρ	λ
0.1	0.0014	-0.71	0.109
0.3	0.0027	0.69	0.107
0.5	0.0020	0.72	0.465

Table 3.5: Representation errors for various utilities for a single risky asset

Panel A: CRRA utility ($\beta = 0.95$)

γ	I_ρ	I_σ	Total	$w_\rho(\%)$	$w_\sigma(\%)$
5	-0.018	-0.323	-0.341	5	95
15	-0.052	-0.282	-0.334	16	84
30	-0.101	-0.223	-0.325	31	69

Panel B: Abel utility ($\beta = 0.95$)

γ	I_ρ	I_σ	Total	$w_\rho(\%)$	$w_\sigma(\%)$
5	-0.019	-0.320	-0.338	6	94
15	-0.060	-0.264	-0.324	19	81
30	-0.129	-0.174	-0.303	42	58

Note: $w_\rho = |I_\rho|/(|I_\rho| + |I_\sigma|)$, $w_\sigma = |I_\sigma|/(|I_\rho| + |I_\sigma|)$.

than the previous three models, it improves both the correlation and the volatility substantially. The correlation ρ is improved from the negative value of -71% to the positive value of 72%, and the volatility ratio λ is improved from 0.109 to 0.465, which is much closer to the optimal volatility ratio of 72%. The structural theory of asset pricing, coupled with the above empirical results, suggests that in order to find a proper SDF, the most important consideration is to determine which set of economic state variables is proper. The next important consideration is to decide on the appropriate functional form for the utility functional for these economic state variables.

3.5.3   Decomposition of the pricing errors

Tables (3.5) - (3.7) show the pricing errors in accordance to the decomposition in Corollary (3.4.2). Again, we can see that the main pricing error is due to a mis-match of the volatilities of two SDFs, as a result of the volatility of consumption staying low (especially after World War II) while the volatility of stocks remaining high. The correlation bias only contributes on average 15% or less to the errors. Comparing the Epstein-Zin model with others, we can see that its correlation bias can be reduced readily if the elasticity of inter-temporal substitution is very small and the coefficient of relative risk aversion is no more than 5.

Table 3.6: Representation errors for various utilities

Panel C1: Constantinides utility $(\beta = 0.95, \gamma = 5)$

φ	I_ρ	I_σ	Total	$w_\rho(\%)$	$w_\sigma(\%)$
0.1	-0.019	-0.321	-0.340	6	94
0.5	-0.033	-0.301	-0.334	10	90
0.9	-0.218	-0.065	-0.283	77	23

Panel C2: Constantinides utility $(\beta = 0.95, \gamma = 15)$

φ	I_ρ	I_σ	Total	$c_\rho(\%)$	$c_\sigma(\%)$
0.1	-0.056	-0.276	-0.332	17	83
0.5	-0.101	-0.213	-0.314	32	68
0.9	-1.872	1.684	-0.188	55	47

Note: $c_\rho = I_\rho/(|I_\rho| + |I_\sigma|)$, $c_\sigma = I_\sigma/(|I_\rho| + |I_\sigma|)$.

Table 3.7: Representation errors for various utilities

Panel D1: Epstein-Zin utility $(\beta = 0.95, \gamma = 5)$

η	I_ρ	I_σ	Total	$c_\rho(\%)$	$c_\sigma(\%)$
0.1	-0.003	-0.303	-0.306	1	99
0.3	-0.090	-0.296	-0.385	23	77
0.5	-0.321	-0.180	-0.501	64	36

Panel D2: Epstein-Zin utility $(\beta = 0.95, \gamma = 15)$

η	I_ρ	I_σ	Total	$c_\rho(\%)$	$c_\sigma(\%)$
0.1	-0.089	-0.277	-0.366	24	76
0.3	-0.543	0.055	-0.598	91	9
0.5	-1.72	0.635	-1.085	73	27

Note: $c_\rho = I_\rho/(|I_\rho| + |I_\sigma|)$, $c_\sigma = I_\sigma/(|I_\rho| + |I_\sigma|)$.

Table 3.8: Representation errors for a portfolio of risky assets (The utility is CRRA with $\beta = 0.95$ and $\gamma = 5$)

Assets	I_ρ	I_σ	$w - v$	$c_\rho(\%)$	$c_\sigma(\%)$
AEP	-0.019	-0.097	-0.117	16	84
GE	0.018	-0.096	0.114	16	84
GM	0.009	0.190	0.199	4	96
IBM	-0.017	-0.156	-0.173	10	90
XOM	-0.007	0.126	0.119	5	95
Average	-0.003	0.032	0.028	1 0	90

Table 3.8 shows the representation errors for a portfolio of five stocks, namely AEP, GE, GM, IBM and XOM, which are all blue chip companies in the U.S. Again we can see that the pricing error given by CRRA's SDF has a small correlation bias, which contributes on average only 10%, but its volatility bias contributes on average 90%. Finally, the GE stock has the smallest volatility bias.

3.6 Conclusions

In this chapter, we have developed further the structural theory for asset pricing modelling. We now have, as a refinement of the SDF theory initiated by Cochran (2001), an 'algebra of operations', with which we can derive pricing models.

The symmetric theorem provides a way to value non-tradable factors, such as economic indices, by reflexively using market assets and their corresponding market prices. The expanding theorem provides a bottom-up way to construct asset pricing models. First we look for correctly pricing SDFs for simpler portfolios in subspaces of an asset space. Second we compound the SDFs into an advanced SDF to price correctly portfolios in the asset space, by removing excessive cross-pricing effects among the SDFs. For example, once we have correctly pricing SDFs domestically, then we can compound them into a single SDF to price international portfolios correctly. The compression theorem provides a top-down way to construct asset pricing models. To price well-diversified asset portfolios with a K-factor structure correctly, a necessary and sufficient condition for the SDF space to have a unique correctly pricing SDF is that the SDF space possesses a K-factor structure as well. In other words, both spaces have no idiosyncratic risk and only K factor risks are left to be considered. Cochrane (2000) has used this fact without giving a rigorous proof. A combination of the expanding theorem and the compression theorem provides us with a routine with which we can value portfolios at different levels. Based on the theory of corporate finance, the theory of interest rate and the theory of derivative pricing, the valuation of an individual security is well developed. However, portfolio valuation, especially risk arbitrage portfolio valuation, well-diversified portfolio valuation or index valuation, is less so. See Cohen (2004) for example. Finally, the pricing error theorem indicates a way to measure how well a given SDF does the pricing job, by first projecting two SDFs (the given SDF and the unknown correctly pricing SDF) into the asset space, and then measuring the distance (using for example the Hansen-Jagannathan distance) between the two projected proxies. Three sources of pricing errors are identified as the differences in the means of the two proxies, the differences in the volatilities of the two proxies, and the imperfect correlation between the two proxies. Our empirical results show that the main contribution to the pricing error is the difference in volatilities.

Chapter 4

Investment and Consumption in a Multi-period Framework

4.1 Review of Merton's Asset Pricing Model

In Merton's multi-period framework (1973), there is no restriction on the consumption beyond its being non-negative. However, not every investor will agree with this lack of restriction. One simple example is to do with endowment funds (Thaler & Williamson, 1994), such as the Nobel Prize fund. There are at least three reasons why the Nobel prize committee would need to impose some consumption discipline. The first is that, every year, a fixed amount of cash is taken out from the fund to provide the Nobel prizes to the winners. The second is that the growth rate of the endowment funds needs to keep abreast of the inflation rate. The third is that it was the wish of Nobel that the Nobel prize fund should last forever.

In the habit models of Abel (1990), Campbell and Cochrane (2000), and many others, it is generally accepted that it is human nature to keep improving one's living standards. If the consumption is below somebody's habit level due to some reason, the person will feel unhappy and attempt to overcome the *relatively* hard time. A reasonable assumption is, in our opinion, to treat the consumption habit as a consumption constraint, $c_t \geq h_t$, where c_t is the consumption level at time t and h_t is the consumption habit at time t.

The relationship between the volatilities of the consumption and the stock markets has attracted attention in recent years. Poterba (2000) finds the 'wealth effect' by examining the relationship between the total consumption and the total wealth of the stock market. His result shows that one US dollar change of the total value of the stock market will bring about one to two cents of change in the consumption. If we assume that the stock market is complete, then the consumption habit is spanned by the portfolios in the stock market.

Financial Model

Let $(\Omega, \mathcal{F}, \mathbb{P})$ be a complete probability space, and $(\mathcal{F}_t)_{0 \leq t \leq T}$ a filtration satisfying the usual conditions. $\mathcal{F}_0 = \sigma\{\emptyset, \Omega\}, \mathcal{F}_T = \mathcal{F}$, where positive number T is a fixed and finite time horizon. We consider a security market which consists of $m + 1$ assets: one bond and m stocks. The price of the risk-free bond at time t is e^{rt}, where r is a non-negative constant. For $j = 1, \cdots, m$, the price of stock j at time t is S_t^j and S^j is a strictly positive semimartingale with càdlàg paths. For notational convenience, we set $S = (S^1, \cdots, S^m)$.

Stochastic integration is used to describe the outcomes of investment strategies. When dealing with processes in dimensions higher than one, it is understood that vector stochastic integration is used. Interested readers may wish to refer to Protter (1990) for details on these matters. We use the notation $\int_0^t H dX$ or $(H.X)_t$ to stand for the integral of H with respect to (or w.r.t. for short) X over the interval $(0, t]$. In particular, $(H.X)_0 = 0$.

A probability measure $\mathbb{Q}$ is called an equivalent martingale measure if it is equivalent to the historical probability measure $\mathbb{P}$ and the discounted price processes of stocks $(e^{-rt}S_t)$ is a (vector-valued) $\mathbb{Q}$-martingale. By $\mathcal{M}$ we denote the set of all equivalent martingale measures. We make the standard assumption that $\mathcal{M}$ is not empty to exclude arbitrage opportunities. The security market is called complete if $\mathcal{M}$ is a singleton, or else we say that the market is incomplete.

We assume that the market is complete and there is a unique probability measure $\mathbb{Q}$, which has a density function $\phi_t = \mathbb{E}\left[\frac{d\mathbb{Q}}{d\mathbb{P}} \mid \mathcal{F}_t\right], t \in [0, T]$, in $\mathcal{M}$.

Trading Strategies

A trading strategy is an $\mathbb{R}^{m+1}$-valued $\mathcal{F}_t$-predictable process $\alpha = \{\alpha^0, \psi\}$, such that ψ is integrable w.r.t. the semi-martingale (S^0, S), where $\psi = (\alpha^1, \cdots, \alpha^m)$ and α_t^j represents the number of units of the asset j held at time t, $0 \leq j \leq m$. The wealth $W_t(\alpha)$ of a trading strategy $\alpha = \{\alpha^0, \psi\}$ at time t is $W_t(\alpha) = \alpha_t^0 S_t^0 + \psi_t \cdot S_t$, where $\psi_t \cdot S_t = \sum_{j=1}^m \alpha_t^j S_t^j$. A trading strategy $\alpha = \{\alpha^0, \psi\}$ is said to be self-financing if

$$dW_t(\alpha) = -c_t dt + \alpha_t d(S_t^0, S_t), t \in [0, T], \tag{4.1}$$

where c_t is the consumption at time t.

It is easy to see that for any given $\mathbb{R}^m$-valued predictable process ψ which is integrable w.r.t. S and any real number x, there exists a real-valued predictable process α^0 such that $\{\alpha^0, \psi\}$ is a self-financing strategy with initial wealth x.

Because we have assumed that the market is complete and there is a unique probability measure $\mathbb{Q}$ in $\mathcal{M}$, every contingent claim in this market, therefore, can be replicated by a self-financing trading strategy.

Inter-temporal Investment and Consumption Problem

The investor endowed with an initial wealth $W_0 > 0$ tries to find the optimal consumption and investment decisions to maximize his total expected utility, i.e.

$$\max_{(c_t, \alpha_t), t \in [0, T]} \mathbb{E}\left(\int_0^T e^{-\rho t} U(c_t) dt\right), \tag{4.2}$$

where ρ is the time preference of consumption and $U(c)$ is the consumption utility function satisfying

- $U(c)$ has continuous second order derivative function on $[0, T]$;

- $U_c = \frac{dU}{dc} > 0, U_{cc} = \frac{d^2 U}{dc^2} < 0$;

- $U_c(0) = \lim_{c \downarrow 0} U_c(c) = \infty, U_c(\infty) = \lim_{c \to \infty} U_c(c) = 0.$

The utility function

$$U(c) = c^\gamma / \gamma \tag{4.3}$$

is called the CRRA (Constant Relative Risk Aversion) utility function.

Consumption Habit Constraints

There exists a real valued $\mathcal{F}_t$-predictable habit consumption process $h_t :$ $[0, T] \times \Omega \to$ satisfying [1]

$$c_t \geq h_t, t \in [0, T]. \tag{4.4}$$

We shall refer to the above inequality as a consumption habit constraint.

---

[1] Hereafter inequality is valid with probability 1.

There are several types of habit process. One broad class is proposed by Detemple and Karatzas (2001), which gives that

$$dh_t = (\delta h_t - \alpha c_t)dt + \delta \eta_t' dB_t, \tag{4.5}$$

where $h_0 \geq 0, \alpha \geq 0, \delta \geq 0$ are given real constants, $\eta_t : [0, T] \times \Omega \to R^m$ is a bounded, progressively measurable process and $B_t = (B_t^1, B_t^2, \cdots, B_t^m)$ is the price driving Brownian process on the probability space $(\Omega, \mathcal{F}, \mathbb{P})$.

If we let $\alpha = 0, \delta \eta_t = h_t \sigma_m$, then the Detemple and Karatzas's habit becomes

$$\frac{dh_t}{h_t} = \mu_m dt + \sigma_m dB_t, \tag{4.6}$$

which is studies in details in Cheng and Wei (2005).

4.2   Optimal Decisions of Investment and Consumption

4.2.1   Martingale approach to the asset pricing model without consumption habit constraints

In this section we review some classic results of Merton's Model, in which there is no consumption habit constraint. Given time-separable preferences defined over consumption and initial wealth $W_0 > 0$, the optimal portfolio and consumption problem without consumption habit is

$$\max_{(c_t, \alpha_t), t \in [0, T]} \mathbb{E} \left(\int_0^T e^{-\rho t} U(c_t) dt \right),$$

with budget constraints given by (4.1).

Martingale Approach

Cox and Huang (1989), Karatzas, Lehoczky and Shreve (1987) and Pliska (1986) have suggested a martingale approach to inter-temporal consumption and portfolio choice that takes advantage of the properties of the stochastic discount factor in a complete market. The martingale method exploits the fact that, under assumptions of no-arbitrage and market completeness, there exists a unique and positive state price ϕ_t satisfying

$$\mathbb{E}_t[\phi_u S_u] = \mathbb{E}\left[\phi_u S_u | \mathcal{F}_t\right] = \phi_t S_t, \quad for \ u > t. \tag{4.7}$$

The process ϕ_t can be interpreted as a system of Arrow-Debreu security. That is, ϕ_t is the claim to one unit of consumption contingent on the occurrence of each state. Then the price of the asset is given by the weighted average of the prices of the payoffs of the states, with each weight being the probability of the relevant state occurring. With the help of ϕ, the Merton's dynamic optimization problem can be changed to a static optimization problem. The budget constraint (4.1) becomes a static budget constraint

$$\mathbb{E}\left[\int_0^T c_t \phi_t dt\right] = \phi_0 W_0, \tag{4.8}$$

which says that the amount the investor allocates to consumption in each state multiplied by the price of consumption in that state must equal his total wealth. By the same reasoning, for any $t \in [0, T]$ and any self-financing trading strategy α, the following equality holds

$$\mathbb{E}\left[\int_t^T c_u \phi_u du \,\middle|\, \mathcal{F}_t\right] = \phi_t W_t(\alpha). \tag{4.9}$$

The optimal consumption is given by

$$c_t^* = U_c^{-1}(\lambda e^{\rho t}\phi_t), t \in [0, T], \tag{4.10}$$

where λ is determined by $\mathbb{E}\left[\int_0^T c_t^* \phi_t dt\right] = \phi_0 W_0$ and U_c^{-1} is the inverse function of U_c.

4.2.2 Martingale approach to the asset pricing model with consumption habit

In this section we discuss the strategies of investors with consumption habit constraints. We will show that the optimal consumption strategies are related with consumption insurance.

The following proposition is the main result, which gives the optimal consumption decision to Merton's problem with consumption habit constraints. Before stating it, we need to guarantee that the initial endowment, W_0 say, is affordable for the future habit consumption; at least the consumption habit constraints should be satisfied. Specifically

$$W_0 \geq \frac{1}{\phi_0}\mathbb{E}\left[\int_0^T \phi_s h_s ds\right], \tag{4.11}$$

where the right-hand side is the total discount value of the future consumption. We say that W_0 is affordable if it satisfies (4.11). From now on we assume that W_0 is affordable.

Proposition 4.2.1 *The optimal consumption is given by*

$$c_t^*(\lambda) = \begin{cases} X_t(\lambda) & if \ \phi_t \leq \phi_t^h(\lambda), \\ h_t & if \ \phi_t > \phi_t^h(\lambda), \end{cases} \qquad (4.12)$$

where $\phi_t^h(\lambda) = U_c(h_t)/\lambda e^{\rho t}$, $X_t(\lambda) = U_c^{-1}(\lambda e^{\rho t}\phi_t)$, $t \in [0,T]$, and $\lambda \geq 0$ is the root of the equation

$$\mathbb{E}\left[\int_0^T \left(X_t(\lambda)\phi_t I_{\{\phi_t \leq \phi_t^h(\lambda)\}} + h_t\phi_t I_{\{\phi_t > \phi_t^h(\lambda)\}}\right) dt\right] = W_0\phi_0. \quad (4.13)$$

Moreover $c_t^*(\lambda)$ can be re-written as

$$c_t^*(\lambda) = \max\left((X_t(\lambda), h_t\right) \qquad (4.14)$$

and correspondingly the optimal wealth process is given by

$$W_t^*(\lambda) = \frac{1}{\phi_t}\mathbb{E}\left[\int_t^T \phi_s \max(X_s(\lambda), h_s)ds \,\middle|\, \mathcal{F}_t\right], \quad t \in [0,T]. \quad (4.15)$$

Sketch of proof: As the full proof is rather long, we give only the key points here. Interested readers can consult Cheng and Wei (2005) for details. First we need a Lemma.

Lemma 4.2.2 *For any given $t \in [0,T]$, let $f(c) = e^{-\rho t}U(c) - \lambda c\phi_t + \eta I_{\{c \geq h_t\}}$, where λ is given by (4.13), and*

$$\eta_t = e^{-\rho t}U(U_c^{-1}(\lambda e^{\rho t}\phi_t)) - \lambda U_c^{-1}(\lambda e^{\rho t}\phi_t)\phi_t - e^{-\rho t}U(h_t) + \lambda h_t\phi_t.$$

Then the function $f(c)$ attains its maximum at c_t^* defined in (4.14), that is,

$$\max_{0 \leq c < \infty} f(c) = f(c_t^*) \qquad (4.16)$$

and $\eta \geq 0$.

We can prove this lemma in two steps. The first step is to prove $\eta \geq 0$. The function f(c) is a corrected concave function, which is moved upwards by η and no longer a concave function with a jump point at $c = c^*$. So a possible candidate for the maximum point will be at $c = c^*$ among other possible candidates. The maximum point will be obtained by comparing these possible candidates. The second step is to prove that c_t^* is the maximum point. We omit the details.

Now, assume that $c_t, t \in [0, T]$, is a strategy satisfying the static budget constraint (4.8) and habit constraint (4.4), so that

$$E\left[\int_0^T c(t)\phi_t dt\right] \leq W_0\phi_0, \tag{4.17}$$

and $c_t \geq h_t, \forall t \in [0, T]$. From the definition of λ we know

$$E\left[\int_0^T c_t^*\phi_t dt\right] = W_0\phi_0. \tag{4.18}$$

Therefore we have

$$E\left[\int_0^T e^{-\rho t}U(c_t^*)dt\right] - E\left[\int_0^T e^{-\rho t}U(c_t)dt\right]$$

$$\geq E\left[\int_0^T e^{-\rho t}U(c_t^*)dt\right] - E\left[\int_0^T e^{-\rho t}U(c_t)dt\right]$$

$$- E\left[\lambda\int_0^T c_t^*\phi_t dt\right] + E\left[\lambda\int_0^T c_t\phi_t dt\right]$$

$$+ E\left[\int_0^T \eta_t I_{\{c_t^* \geq h_t\}}dt\right] - E\left[\int_0^T \eta_t I_{\{c_t \geq h_t\}}dt\right]$$

$$= E\left[\int_0^T (f(c_t^*) - f(c_t))dt\right] \geq 0 \tag{4.19}$$

Remark 4.2.3 *From (4.10) we know that $X_s(\lambda)$ is actually the optimal consumption process without the consumption habit constraint (4.4). The* *optimal wealth process (4.15) can be re-written as*

$$W_t^* = \frac{1}{\phi_t}\mathbb{E}\left[\int_t^T \phi_s \max(X_s, h_s)ds\,\bigg|\,\mathcal{F}_t\right]$$

$$= \int_t^T e^{-r(s-t)}\mathbb{E}_{\mathbb{Q}}[h_s|\mathcal{F}_t]ds$$

$$+ \int_t^T e^{-r(s-t)}\mathbb{E}_{\mathbb{Q}}[\max(X_s - h_s, 0)|\mathcal{F}_t]ds. \qquad (4.20)$$

In words, the optimally invested wealth at time t is composed of two parts, one part being the wealth which finances the habit consumption in the future after time t, another being the total cost of a consecutive set of call options of the process $\{X_u, u \in [t, T]\}$ with the stochastic striking price $h_s \in [t, T]$ at time s.

Remark 4.2.4 *Let us consider again Merton's problem with a different initial endowment $W_u \leq W_0$. In the above subsection, we have stated that the optimal consumption process is*

$$c_{u,t}^*(\lambda_u) = U_c^{-1}(\lambda_u e^{\rho t}\phi_t),$$

where λ_u is the root of the equation

$$\mathbb{E}\left[\int_0^T c_{u,t}^*(\lambda_u)\phi_t dt\right] = \phi_0 W_u.$$

Then λ_u is a function of the initial endowment W_u. Therefore if W_u is suitably chosen we can make $\lambda_u = \lambda$ and then the process $X_s(\lambda) = U_c^{-1}(\lambda e^{\rho t}\phi_t)$ is the same as the optimal consumption process $c_{u,t}^*(\lambda_u)$; that is $X_t(\lambda) = c_{u,t}^*(\lambda_u)$. From now on we will call $X_t, t \in [0, T]$, the optimal consumption process of a relevant Merton's problem with a relevant initial endowment W_u. It is easy to see that $W_u \leq W_0$ because $c_t^* \geq c_{u,t}^*$.

4.3   Optimal Investment Behavior

In this section we study the optimal investment behavior of an investor with consumption habit constraints and without labour income. We will see that the portfolio insurance strategy plays a central role in the consumption shortfall risk; the benchmark of a shortfall in the consumption is the consumption habit.

For simplicity of explanation, we assume that the market consists of just two assets (i.e. m=2), one being a risky asset that prices according to the geometric Brownian dynamics $dS_t = \mu S_t dt + \sigma S_t dB_t$, another being a riskless asset that earns a constant instantaneous rate of interest, $r > 0$, so that $dR_t = rR_t dt, R_0 > 0$. In this case, the dynamics of the state price density is

$$d\phi_t = -r\phi_t dt - \kappa \phi_t dB_t, \tag{4.21}$$

where $\kappa = \sigma^{-1}(\mu - r)$. The budget constraint (4.1) becomes

$$dW_t = [\alpha_t W_t(\mu - r) + W_t r - c_t]dt + \alpha_t W_t \sigma dB_t. \tag{4.22}$$

The general utility

Proposition 4.3.1 *Assume that the optimal wealth process W_t^* can be expressed as a function of $\{S_t, \phi_t, h_t\}$, so that there exists a function $f(t, x, y, z)$ satisfying $W_t^* = f(t, S_t, \phi_t, h_t)$. Assume that f has continuous second-order derivatives with respects to $\{t, x, y, z\}$. Then the demand for the risky asset by the investor with Detemple and Karatzas' consumption habit (4.5) is given by*

$$\alpha_t^* = \frac{S_t f_x}{W_t^*} - \frac{\phi_t f_y}{W_t^*}\kappa\sigma^{-1} + \frac{\eta_t f_z}{W_t^*}\sigma^{-1}\delta. \tag{4.23}$$

Proof: By Ito Lemma we have

$$dW_t^* = \left(\mathcal{L}f + f_t\right)dt + \left(f_x S_t \sigma + f_y Z_t \kappa + f_z \delta\eta_t\right)dB_t, \tag{4.24}$$

where $\mathcal{L}$ denotes the Merton differential generator of (S, ϕ, h) under P. (Lemma 5.1 in Merton (1990).) At the same time the optimal consumption and the optimal portfolio satisfy the budget constraint (4.22). The demand for risky asset is obtained by comparing the coefficients of the stochastic parts of (4.22) and (4.24) and the uniqueness of the Itô's process.

Q.E.D.

In words, the proposition says that after adding the consumption habit constraint, the demand for risky asset becomes

demand for risky asset = myopic demand based on asset's
risk premium

+ hedge demand against adverse change
in investment opportunity

+ hedge demand against adverse
consumption with change of wealth.

$$(4.25)$$

The CRRA utility

In order to gain further insights on how consumption habit constraints affect the investment behavior, we specify the utility to be a CRRA utility of the form (4.3) and consumption habit as (4.6). For a general utility as discussed in the last section, the effect of the consumption habit constraint is that the optimal investment decision needs to hedge adverse consumption with change of wealth.

Proposition 4.3.2 *The optimal wealth process of an investor with the consumption habit* (4.6) *is given by*

$$W_t^* = W_t^g + W_t^f, \qquad (4.26)$$

where

$$W_t^g = X_t \int_0^{T-t} e^{-\tilde{r}u} N(d_1(u)) du,$$

$$W_t^f = h_t \int_0^{T-t} e^{-\tilde{\mu}_m u} \left(1 - N(d_2)\right) du, \qquad (4.27)$$

$$\tilde{r} = \frac{\rho}{1-\gamma} - \frac{\gamma}{1-\gamma}\left(r + \frac{\kappa^2}{2(1-\gamma)}\right), \qquad (4.28)$$

$$\sigma_y = \frac{1}{1-\gamma}\kappa - \sigma_m, \quad \tilde{\mu}_m = r + \sigma_m \kappa - \mu_m, \qquad (4.29)$$

$$d_1(u) = \frac{\log\left(X_t/h_t\right) + (\tilde{\mu}_m - \tilde{r} + \sigma_y^2/2)u}{\sigma_y \sqrt{u}}, \qquad (4.30)$$

$$d_2(u) = d_1(u) - \sigma_y \sqrt{u}, \qquad (4.31)$$

$$X_t = \left(e^{-\rho t}/\phi_t\right)^{1/(1-\gamma)} \qquad (4.32)$$

and $N(\cdot)$ *is the standard normal distribution.*

Proof: Let

$$\frac{d\mathbb{Q}}{d\mathbb{P}}\bigg|\,\mathcal{F}_T = exp\left(-\kappa B_t - \frac{1}{2}\kappa^2 t\right), \quad \frac{d\mathbb{Q}_Y}{d\mathbb{Q}}\bigg|\,\mathcal{F}_T = \frac{e^{-rT}Y_T}{Y_0}. \tag{4.33}$$

Let $u \in [t,T]$ and $s \in [t,u]$. Define $Z_t \triangleq 1/\phi_t$, $\mu_m^* = \mu_m - \sigma_m\kappa$ and $Y_s = e^{-\mu_m^*(s-u)}h_s$, which has the same terminal payoff as h_s at time u and is a martingale under measure $\mathbb{Q}$. Therefore we have

$$e^{-r(u-t)}\mathbb{E}_\mathbb{Q}[h_u|\mathcal{F}_t] = e^{-r(u-t)}\mathbb{E}_\mathbb{Q}[h_u|\mathcal{F}_t] = e^{(\mu_m^*-r)(u-t)}h_t. \tag{4.34}$$

It is easy to see that $U_c^{-1}(x) = x^{-1/(1-\gamma)}$. Now, let $X_s = U_c^{-1}(e^{\rho s}Z_s^{-1}) = \left(e^{-\rho u}Z_s\right)^{1/(1-\gamma)}$, $\hat{X}_s = \frac{X_s}{Y_s}$. By Itô's Formula and according to (4.21) we have

$$\frac{d\hat{X}_s}{\hat{X}_s} = \left(r^* + \sigma_m^2 - \frac{1}{1-\gamma}\sigma_m\kappa\right)ds + \sigma_y dB_s^\mathbb{Q}$$

$$= r^*ds + \sigma_y dB_s^{\mathbb{Q}_Y}, \tag{4.35}$$

where $\sigma_y = \frac{1}{1-\gamma}\kappa - \sigma_m$ and $r^* = \frac{1}{1-\gamma}(r + \frac{\gamma}{2(1-\gamma)}\kappa^2 - \rho)$.

Now, let $\bar{X}_s = e^{-r^*(s-u)}\hat{X}_s$, which has the same payoff function as $\hat{X}_s$ at the terminal time u. From (4.35) and by Itô's Lemma we know that $\bar{X}_s$ is a $\mathbb{Q}_Y$-martingale and the mean part is zero. By the Black-Scholes formula, the value of a call option with underlying price process $\bar{X}_s$, striking price 1 and riskless return rate 0 under martingale measure $\mathbb{Q}_Y$ is

$$\mathbb{E}_{\mathbb{Q}_Y}\left(\max(\hat{X}_s - 1, 0)\big|\,\mathcal{F}_t\right) = \mathbb{E}_{\mathbb{Q}_Y}\left(\max(\bar{X}_s - 1, 0)\big|\,\mathcal{F}_t\right)$$

$$= \bar{X}_t N(d_1) - N(d_2),$$

where

$$\hat{X}_t = e^{-r^*(t-u)}\hat{X}_t = \frac{e^{-r^*(t-u)}\left(e^{-\rho t}/\phi_t\right)^{1/(1-\gamma)}}{e^{\mu_m^*(u-t)}h_t}. \tag{4.36}$$

After some tedious calculations, the proof of the proposition is completed.

Q.E.D.

Proposition 4.3.3 *The demand for the risky asset at time t by the investor with Cheng and Wei's consumption habit (4.6) is given by*

$$\alpha_t^* = \frac{\sigma^{-1}\kappa}{1-\gamma}\alpha_t^g + \sigma^{-1}\sigma_m\alpha_t^f \tag{4.37}$$

$$= \alpha_t^M + H_t, \tag{4.38}$$

where

$$\alpha_t^g = W_t^g/W_t^*, \quad \alpha_t^f = W_t^f/W_t^*, \tag{4.39}$$

$$H_t = -\sigma^{-1}\left(\frac{\kappa}{1-\gamma} - \sigma_m\right)\alpha_t^f, \tag{4.40}$$

σ_y, W_t^g, W_t^f *are defined as in Proposition* (4.3.2) *and* $\alpha_t^M = \frac{\sigma^{-1}\kappa}{1-\gamma}$.

Proof: From result (4.26) it is not difficult to get

$$\left(e^{-\rho t}/\phi_t\right)^{\frac{1}{1-\gamma}} e^{-\tilde{r}u} n(d_1) - h_t e^{-\tilde{\mu}_m u} n(d_2) = 0, \tag{4.41}$$

where $n(.)$ is the density function of a standard Normal distribution. By direct calculations and using the above equation, we have

$$W_Z^* Z = \frac{1}{1-\gamma} W_t^g, \quad W_h^* h = W_t^f. \tag{4.42}$$

Substituting the above equations in (4.23) and using the fact that the optimal wealth is independent of the price processes we get our result.

Q.E.D.

As indicated in the comments after Proposition (4.3.2), we call α_t^g a *growth wealth ratio* and α_t^f a *floor wealth ratio*.

Remark 4.3.4 *Let us examine again the investment strategy* (4.37). *We can re-write it as*

$$\alpha_t^* W_t^* = \frac{\sigma^{-1}\kappa}{1-\gamma}(W_t^* - W_t^f) + \sigma^{-1}\sigma_m W_t^f$$

$$= I_1 + I_2. \tag{4.43}$$

In other words, the optimal investment strategy is a combination of two strategies, the first one being the famous strategy CPPI (Constant Proportion Portfolio Insurance-Leland and Rubinstein, 1986). If $\sigma_m = 0$, then the investment strategy becomes a CPPI strategy with $m = \kappa/(1-\gamma)$, showing the risk aversion of the investor. The second strategy is also needed because the consumption habit is uncertain too due to $\sigma_m \neq 0$; in other words, the investor will take the chance of investing more by being willing to have possible lower consumption habit. The investors can lower their risk aversion if they are willing to lower their living standard.

4.4 Conclusions

In this chapter we first argue that for a large group of investors, their port-folio and consumption choice problem must be linked to the consumption habit constraint. For this new choice problem, by using the Cox and Huang martingale approach, we can obtain an optimal wealth path and demand for risky assets under a general utility. In the case of some special habits and under the CRRA utility, analytic solutions are obtained. Furthermore we have arrived at two interesting and important conclusions: (1) Beyond the Merton's decomposition formula for investor's demand for risky asset, the demand has a third component to hedge against adverse change of consumption such as the willingness (or reluctance) to maintain the living standard, and others. (2) After imposing the consumption habit require-ment, even for the CRRA utility, the investor's optimal strategy is related to the CPPI strategy.

Bibliography

[1] Abel, AB (1990). Asset prices under habit formation and catching up with the Jones. *American Economic Review Papers and Proceedings*, 80, 38–42.

[2] Aiyagari, SR and M Gertler (1991). Asset Returns with Transactions Costs and Uninsured Individual Risk. *Journal of Monetary Economics*, 27, 311–331.

[3] Alvarez, F and U Jermann (2000). Efficiency, equilibrium, and asset pricing with risk of default. *Econometrica*, 68, 775–797.

[4] Bansal, R and JW Coleman (1996). A monetary explanation of the equity premium, term premium and risk free asset rate puzzles. *Journal of Political Economy*, 104, 1135–1171.

[5] Bossaerts, P (2002). *The Paradox of Asset Pricing*. Princeton, NJ: Princeton University Press.

[6] Brav, A, GM Constantinides and CC Geczy (2002). Asset pricing with heterogeneous consumers and limited participation: Empirical evidence. *Journal of Political Economy*, 110, 793–824.

[7] Breeden, DT (1979). An intertemporal asset pricing model with stochastic consumption and investment opportunities. *Journal of Financial Economics*, 7, 265–296.

[8] Brown, S, W Goetzmann and S Ross (1995). Survival. *Journal of Finance*, 50, 853–873.

[9] Campbell, JY and JH Cochrane (1999). By force of habit: A consumption-based explanation of aggregate stock market behavior. *Journal of Political Economy*, 107, 205–251.

[10] Campbell, JY and JH Cochrane (2000). Explaining the poor performance of consumption-based asset pricing models. *Journal of Finance*, 55, 2863–2878.

[11] Campbell, JY and ML Viceira (2002). *Strategic Asset Allocation — Portfolio Choice for Long-Term Investors*. Clarendon Lectures in Economics, London: Oxford University Press.

[12] Chamberlain, G (1983). Funds, factors, and diversification in arbitrage pricing models. *Econometrica*, 51, 1305–1323.

[13] Chamberlain, G and M Rothschild (1983). Arbitrage, factor structure, and mean-variance analysis. *Econometrica*, 51, 1281–1304.

[14] Cheng, B and X Wei (2005). Portfolio and consumption decisions with consumption habit constraints. *Nonlinear Analysis*, 63, 2335–2346.

[15] Cochrane, JH (2000). *Asset Pricing*. Princeton, New Jersey: Princeton University Press.

[16] Cochrane, JH (2001). *Asset Pricing*. Princeton, New Jersey: Princeton University Press.

[17] Cohen, RD (2004). An objective approach to relative valuation. Working paper, the Citigroup.

[18] Constantinides, GM (1990). Habit formation: A resolution of the equity premium puzzle. *Journal of Political Economy*, 98, 519–543.

[19] Constantinides, GM and D Duffie (1996). Asset pricing with heterogeneous consumers. *Journal of Political Economy*, 104, 219–240.

[20] Constantinides, GM, JB Donaldson and R Mehra (2002). Junior Cant Borrow: A new perspective on the equity premium puzzle. *Quarterly Journal of Economics*, 117, 269–296.

[21] Cox, JC and C Huang (1989). Optimum consumption and portfolio policies when asset prices follow a diffusion process. *Journal of Economic Theory*, 49, 33–83.

[22] Detemple, J and I Karatzas (2001). Non-Additive Habits: Optimal Consumption Portfolio Policies, Working Paper.

[23] Epstein, LG and SE Zin (1989). Substitution, risk aversion, and the temporal behavior of consumption growth and asset returns I: A theoretical framework. *Econometrica*, 57, 937–969.

[24] Epstein, LG and SE Zin (1991). Substitution, risk aversion, and the temporal behavior of consumption and asset returns II: An empirical analysis. *Journal of Political Economy*, 99, 263–286.

[25] Friedman, M (1957). *A Theory of the Consumption Function*. Princeton: Princeton University Press.

[26] Grossman, S and RJ Shiller (1981). The determinants of the variability of stock market prices. *American Economic Review*, 71, 222–227.

[27] Hall, RE (1978). Stochastic implications of the life cycle-permanent income hypothesis: Theory and evidence. *Journal of Political Economy*, 86, 971–987.

[28] Hansen, LP and HJ Singleton (1982). Generalized instrumental vari-

ables estimation of nonlinear rational expectations models. *Econometrica*, 50, 1269–1286.

[29] Hansen, LP and HJ Singleton (1983). Stochastic consumption, risk aversion, and the temporal behavior of asset returns. *Journal of Political Economy*, 91, 249–265.

[30] Hansen, LP and HJ Singleton (1992). Computing Semiparametric Efficiency Bounds for Linear Time Series Models. In *Nonparametric and Semiparametric Methods in Econometrics and Statistics: Proceedings of the 5th International Symposium in Economic Theory and Econometrics*, WA Barnett, J Powell and GE Tauchen (eds.), pp. 387–412. New York and Melbourne: Cambridge University Press.

[31] Hansen, LP and R Jagannathan (1991). Restrictions on intertemporal marginal rates of substitution implied by asset returns. *Journal of Political Economy*, 99, 225–262.

[32] Hansen, LP and R Jagannathan (1997). Assessing specification errors in stochastic discount factor models. *Journal of Finance*, 52, 557–590.

[33] Heaton, J and DJ Lucas (1996). Evaluating the effects of incomplete markets on risk sharing and asset pricing. *Journal of Political Economy*, 104, 443–487.

[34] Karatzas, I, JP Lehoczky and SE Shreve (1987) Optimal portfolio and consumption decisions for a small investor on a finite horizon. *SIAM Journal of Control and Optimization*, 25, 1557–1586.

[35] Kocherlakota, NR (1996). The equity premium: It is still a puzzle. *Journal of Economic Literature*, 34, 42–71.

[36] Kreps, DM (1981). Arbitrage and equilibrium in economies with infinitely many commodities. *Journal of Mathematical Economics*, 8, 15–35.

[37] Lax, PD (2002). *Functional Analysis.* New York: John Wiley & Sons.

[38] Leland, HE and M Rubinstein (1986). The Evolution of Portfolio Insurance. In *Dynamic Hedging: A Guide to Portfolio Insurance*, D Luskin (ed.), 32–65. New York: John-Wiley and Sons.

[39] Lucas, RE Jr (1976). Econometric policy evaluation: A critique. In *The Phillips Curve and Labor Markets*, Carnegie-Rochester Conference Series on Public Policy 1, K Brunner and A Meltzer (ed.). Amsterdam: North-Holland.

[40] Lucas, RE Jr (1978). Asset pricing in an exchange economy. *Econometrica*, 46, 1429–1445.

[41] Lucas, DJ (1994). Asset pricing with undiversifiable income risk and

short sales constraints deepening the equity premium puzzle. *Journal of Monetary Economics*, 34, 325–341.

[42] Markowitz, H (1952). Portfolio selection. *Journal of Finance*, 7, 77–91.

[43] Mankiw, NG (1986). The equity premium and the concentration of aggregate shocks. *Journal of Financial Economics*, 17, 211–219.

[44] McGrattan, ER and EC Prescott (2001). Taxes, Regulations and Asset Prices. NBER Working Paper No. W8623.

[45] Mehra, R (2003). The Equity Premium: Why is it a Puzzle? Working Paper, No. W9512, National Bureau of Economic Research.

[46] Mehra, R and EC Prescott (1985). The equity premium: A puzzle. *Journal of Monetary Economics*, 15, 145–161.

[47] Merton, CR (1973). An intertemporal capital asset pricing model. *Econometrica*, 41, 867–887.

[48] Merton, CR (1990). *Continuous Time Finance*. Cambridge: Basil Blackwell.

[49] Modigliani, F and R Brumberg (1954). Utility analysis and the consumption function: An interpretation of cross-section data. In *Post-Keynesian Economics*, KK Kurihara (ed.), New Brunswick: Rutgers University Press.

[50] Pliska, SR (1986). A stochastic calculus model of continuous trading: Optimal portfolio. *Mathematics of Operations Research*, 11, 239–246.

[51] Poterba, JM (2000). Stock market wealth and consumption. *Journal of Economic Perspectives*, 14, 99–118.

[52] Protter, PE (1990). Stochastic Integration and Differential Equations. New York: Springer.

[53] Rietz, TA (1988). The equity risk premium: A solution. *Journal of Monetary Economics*, 22, 117–131.

[54] Ross, S (1976). The arbitrage theory of capital asset pricing. *Journal of Economic Theory*, 13, 341–360.

[55] Thaler, RH and JP Williamson (1994). College and university endowment funds: Why not 100% equities? *The Journal of Portfolio Management*, Fall 1994, 27–37.

[56] Telmer, C (1993). Asset pricing puzzles and incomplete markets. *Journal of Finance*, 49, 1803–1832.

[57] Weil, P (1990). Nonexpected utility in macroeconomics. *Quarterly Journal of Economics*, 105, 29–42.

Index